As one of the world's longest established
and best-known travel brands,
Thomas Cook are the experts in travel.

For more than 135 years our
guidebooks have unlocked the secrets
of destinations around the world,
sharing with travellers a wealth of
experience and a passion for travel.

**Rely on Thomas Cook as your
travelling companion on your next trip
and benefit from our unique heritage.**

Thomas Cook **pocket** guides

AMSTERDAM
Mike Gerrard

Your travelling companion since 1873

Thomas
Cook

Written and updated by Mike Gerrard
Original photography by Neil Setchfield

Published by Thomas Cook Publishing
A division of Thomas Cook Tour Operations Limited
Company registration no. 3772199 England
The Thomas Cook Business Park, Unit 9, Coningsby Road,
Peterborough PE3 8SB, United Kingdom
Email: books@thomascook.com, Tel: +44 (0) 1733 416477
www.thomascookpublishing.com

Produced by Cambridge Publishing Management Limited
Burr Elm Court, Main Street, Caldecote CB23 7NU
www.cambridgepm.co.uk

ISBN: 978-1-84848-499-3

© 2006, 2009 Thomas Cook Publishing
This third edition © 2011
Text © Thomas Cook Publishing,
Maps © Thomas Cook Publishing/PCGraphics (UK) Limited
Transport map © Communicarta Limited

Series Editor: Karen Beaulah
Production/DTP: Steven Collins

Printed and bound in Spain by GraphyCems

Cover photography © Perseo Medusa/Shutterstock

CONTENTS

SYMBOLS KEY

The following symbols are used throughout this book:

ⓐ address ☎ telephone ⓦ website address ⓛ opening times
Ⓝ public transport connections ❶ important

The following symbols are used on the maps:

𝒊 information office		▪ point of interest
✈ airport		— railway
✚ hospital		
🛡 police station		
🚌 bus station		
🚆 railway station		
Ⓜ metro		
✝ cathedral		
❶ numbers denote featured cafés & restaurants		

Hotels and restaurants are graded by approximate price as follows:
£ budget price **££** mid-range price **£££** expensive

▶ *The National Monument in Dam Square*

INTRODUCING
Amsterdam

Introduction

A living, breathing city that has always attracted outsiders – be they tourists, philosophers, hippies or immigrants – Amsterdam has great and enduring charm. Its population, currently around 780,000, is small compared to that of most capital cities but its people are as cosmopolitan and forward-thinking as anywhere in the world.

The correct name for the country of which Amsterdam is the capital is the Netherlands. Although people often call it Holland, they are mistakenly referring to the actual province, North Holland, in which the city is located.

What makes the city unique is a combination of both its beauty and its people. Amsterdam's canals, lined with lofty buildings, criss-crossed by simple little bridges and traversed by hundreds of cyclists, are something truly special. They may not be as grand as those of Venice, but you can enjoy them on a much more human scale.

The Dutch people have always been known for their tolerance, and Amsterdam is a city in which you can relax. Unfortunately for those who would like to take a puff in Amsterdam's famous cannabis cafés or coffeshops, a blanket smoking ban inside all public spaces (including hotels) now means that smokers are generally relegated to designated enclosed smoking areas which staff cannot enter. Some coffeeshops allow customers to light a joint outside on the terrace, while others even insist that you do not mix tobacco with your cannabis. It's always best to enquire about the policy upheld at whichever coffeeshop you enter. Many are now becoming private members' clubs in order to discourage drugs tourists.

As bright and brash as ever, the city's infamous red light district continues to draw curiosity seekers as well as some rather less desirable characters to its neon lights and extravagant displays.

But there's far more to Amsterdam than notorious pursuits. It has two of the finest art museums in the world, the Rijksmuseum and the Van Gogh Museum, not to mention Rembrandt's original house and studio. The Anne Frank House, where the Frank family hid from the Nazis during World War II, makes for a powerful and sobering visit.

Above and beyond its attractions, though, Amsterdam is a city all about atmosphere, brown bars and cafés, cheap and cheerful Indonesian restaurants, street markets, quirky shops and friendly locals.

▲ *Amsterdam is easier to get around by foot or bicycle*

When to go

There's no doubt that Amsterdam is a summer city, even though the weather may not always be as summery as you might like. Most people visit from April to October, with the biggest influx during the July and August school holidays. To catch the sun and avoid the crowds, try to go in spring or autumn. Winter can also be atmospheric, and it's a great place for Christmas shopping, as long as you remember to wrap up warm.

SEASONS & CLIMATE

Summers are generally mild and winters can be cold and damp. It seldom gets very hot in the city, even in the height of summer, although it can be rather sticky if it does. It's unlikely the canals will completely freeze again in winter, as they did in 1998, even if they occasionally do in part. It can rain at any time of year. What's more, if the temperature drops, the canals can add an extra chill, so pack with that in mind. But be prepared for anything, all year round – pocket-sized umbrellas and extra layers are key.

ANNUAL EVENTS

If you don't mind a crowd, book early for the best party in town: the Queen's official birthday at the end of April. The city is packed with visitors of all nationalities, mostly dressed in the national colour of orange, and the event is like an extraordinary all-day flea market. August is also the time for crowds, celebrations, music and dance, including the Gay Pride Boat Parade and the excellent Uitmarkt theatre festival.

For up-to-date information on current festivals and events, call the tourist office (see page 152) or check Ⓦ www.amsterdam.info/events or Ⓦ www.iamsterdam.com

February
Carnival takes place every year in the Brabant region, roughly two hours from Amsterdam. The weather doesn't quite rival Rio's, but there is a buzz about the place and a lot of action on the streets.

⬣ *National Windmill Day in May sees windmills in action countrywide*

April–May

National Museum Weekend Free or reduced entry to the country's great art museums. There are also special events and exhibitions. Usually around the first or second weekend of April.

Koninginnedag (Queen's Day) The biggest and best celebration in Amsterdam, held on 30 April. Book accommodation far in advance.

National Windmill Day Amsterdam's windmills (as well as others all over the country) are opened up and the sails set working. What could be more Dutch than this? The event usually takes place on the second Saturday in May.

July–August

Amsterdam Pride Gay Pride celebration at the start of August, including a unique Gay Pride Boat Parade on the canals. The streets are packed and you should expect to see some extravagant outfits and outrageous behaviour. Ⓦ www.amsterdamgaypride.nl

De Parade Travelling theatre festival, offering a wonderful mix of art, theatre, music and food. The festival has been going strong for 15 years. Shows last anything from five minutes to an hour – just show up and buy tickets on the festival grounds. Ⓦ www.deparade.nl

Grachtenfestival (Canal festival) is a classical music festival that sees internationally renowned musicians performing along the river and canals. It's usually held in mid-August. Ⓦ www.grachten festival.nl

September

Open Monumentendag (Open Monuments Day) usually takes place on the second Saturday in September. Many private historical buildings in the city throw open their doors to the public, often free of charge, for an exclusive visit. Ⓦ www.openmonumentendag.nl

Robodock A spectacularly inventive multimedia festival held within an industrial backdrop, Robodok brings together international designers, architects, theatrical performers, musicians and robots. Usually held mid-September. ⓦ www.robodock.org

November–January

Sinterklaas St Nicholas is not Santa Claus but a Turkish saint who loved children. His arrival with his Moorish helper Zwarte Piet (supposedly by boat from Spain) signals the start of the celebrations leading up to Sinterklaas. At this festival on 5 December children receive presents, traditionally found in their shoes.
ⓦ www.stnicholascenter.org

New Year One of Europe's biggest celebrations in one of its most compact cities. Beware the local custom of throwing fireworks.

PUBLIC HOLIDAYS
New Year's Day 1 Jan
Good Friday 6 Apr 2012, 29 Mar 2013, 8 Apr 2014
Easter Sunday & Monday 8 & 9 Apr 2012, 31 Mar & 1 Apr 2013, 10 & 11 Apr 2014
Koninginnedag (Queen's Day) 30 Apr
Ascension Day 17 May 2012, 9 May 2013, 29 May 2014
Pentecost Sunday & Monday 27 & 28 May 2012, 19 & 20 May 2013, 8 & 9 Jun 2014
Christmas & Boxing Day 25 & 26 Dec

Businesses, including some shops and restaurants, are usually closed on Remembrance Day (4 May) and Liberation Day (5 May).

The Heineken story

Heineken hasn't been made in Amsterdam since 1988, when the city brewery closed. It later became the Heineken Experience (see page 84). Heineken is part of the national consciousness: on average, the Dutch consume 69 litres (121 pints) of beer per person every year, much of it Heineken.

It was 1863 when Gerard Adriaan Heineken, a 22-year-old Dutch entrepreneur, bought the brewery that overlooks the Singelgracht canal in Amsterdam. The brewery had been going steady since 1592.

● *Allow a couple of hours for a tour of the old Heineken brewery*

He changed its name from *De Hooiberg* (The Haystack) to his family name and began putting his time and energy into making Dutch beer into a huge export business. Ask for a beer in any continental European country now and you'll often be offered a choice of Heineken or Amstel, both Dutch brews. It's an impressive feat, considering brewing has always been more traditionally linked with countries such as Germany, Belgium and the UK.

Within five years of Heineken buying The Haystack, several other breweries had opened in the city. He cleverly stayed ahead of the competition by buying bars and hotels, to ensure his brew had guaranteed outlets. In 1874 Heineken expanded to Rotterdam with a state-of-the-art brewery. Quality took precedence over price and word of mouth proved more successful than advertising, leading to a reputation for a consistently good brew. Soon Heineken was the biggest exporter of beer to Paris, which at the end of the 19th century was developing rapidly as the most important city in Europe. Throughout this time he kept it as his family business and it remains so to this day.

Ironically, it was Heineken's success that led to the original brewery in Amsterdam being closed in 1988. Production had expanded so much that it was increasingly difficult to get large delivery lorries through the narrow streets. The old shire horses delivering beer locally may have looked picturesque, but they couldn't keep up with the number of bottles needing to be transported, or the huge demand for exports. By 1989 Heineken had become the largest brewer in Europe, the second largest in the world and the biggest exporter of beer to the USA. The beer has won many international prizes over the years.

The Heineken Experience (see page 84), was opened in the former brewery in 2001, and is now one of the city's most popular attractions.

History

Amsterdam's name comes from the dam built by fishermen at the mouth of the Amstel river in the early 13th century. They built their homes on top of small mounds and the fishing village of Amstelledamme was born.

In the 14th century the community flourished as a centre of trade and the first canals were dug. In 1602 the Dutch East India Company was founded. It became hugely successful through its spice trade with Asia and by the end of the 17th century Amsterdam was the biggest port in the world. Amsterdam's Canal Ring was built, in effect turning the city into a series of islands connected by bridges.

In 1806 Napoleon Bonaparte conquered the Netherlands and declared his brother Louis the new king. His reign didn't last. By 1813 the Dutch had regained their independence and William I his throne.

The discovery of diamond fields at the end of the 19th century in South Africa, then part of the Dutch Empire, has made Amsterdam a world centre for diamond trading.

During World War I the Netherlands maintained its independence, but it was occupied by German forces from 1940–45 in World War II.

HERRING
Amsterdam owes its existence to herring. Fisherman had always trawled these waters for herring, but a permanent settlement only came into existence when they learned how to preserve the fish so that more could be brought ashore, processed and sold. The original settlement was actually in what is still the centre of Amsterdam life, Dam Square.

The turbulent 1960s saw Amsterdam gain a reputation as the radical heart of Europe for its tolerance of soft drugs, its politically active youth and the widespread squatting caused by a housing shortage. Immigrants from Suriname, Turkey and Morocco started flocking to the city in the 1980s, attracted by a burgeoning service industry.

As the new century dawned, social problems such as ethnic and sexual discrimination increased and religious differences – as sometimes occur in multi-ethnic, multi-faith communities – began to emerge. In 2001 gay marriage was legalised, though there was strong opposition from fundamentalist religious groups. In 2004 the murder of media celebrity Theo van Gogh, killed by a young Moroccan radical, quickly proved that Amsterdam's famed multiculturalism and tolerance was facing a severe test. Things have calmed in recent years and the city continues to attract tourists for its beauty, architecture, canals and, above all, progressive attitude.

⬤ *Herring is still a popular snack in Amsterdam*

Lifestyle

One word describes the city's vibe: *gezellig*. It roughly translates as cosy, but signifies everything that makes Amsterdam and its people feel relaxed, comfortable, snug and happy. *Gezellig* is how Amsterdammers describe an evening spent in the company of friends and how they feel about making new friends. *Gezellig* is how you will feel in Amsterdam, in a warm bar on a cold night after a couple of drinks, with music in the background and easy conversation all around.

The Dutch are stylish but, unlike the residents of many modern cities, Amsterdammers are not overly fashion-conscious or neurotic. They are happy to travel around on bicycles – and the most basic of bicycles at that. You are more likely to see an achingly beautiful young woman or a smartly suited businessman cycling by on a

⬇ *One of Amsterdam's many brown bars*

sit-up-and-beg boneshaker than a designer bicycle. For Amsterdammers, the point is to get where they want to go.

This relaxed attitude and lifestyle melds well with the city's reputation for tolerance. But don't be fooled. Tolerance has its rules and limits and Amsterdam is in no way anarchistic. You can smoke small amounts of cannabis in some coffeeshops, but don't make a nuisance of yourself while puffing away brazenly in the street. If you do, you'll find the police aren't quite so *gezellig* after all.

Prices are fairly reasonable here, too. The cost of living is about average for northern Europe, perhaps a touch cheaper than London or Paris, but not dramatically so. Hotels are expensive, so visit at quieter times of the year or start your search early for a special deal if you are on a budget. One great advantage of Amsterdam is that you won't need to shell out on taxis or public transport. The city is compact enough for you to stroll around the central canal hub in an hour.

Culture

Amsterdam is one of the world's great art cities. Two men are, for the most part, responsible for this: Rembrandt and Van Gogh. Rembrandt was 25 when he came to Amsterdam in 1631. He lived there until his death in 1669, and you can visit his house and the studio in which he painted, the **Museum Het Rembrandthuis** (see page 69). Some of his major works are also on display in the **Rijksmuseum** (see page 96).

Combine Rembrandt's work with the greatest Van Gogh collection in the world and there's reason enough for art lovers to visit Amsterdam. The **Van Gogh Museum** is one of the city's most visited attractions (see page 98). The **Stedelijk**, Amsterdam's modern art museum (see page 100), also houses unusual and provocative works by some of the world's great names.

If classical music and dance are more your cultural scene, check out the **Concertgebouw** (see page 96) where the Dutch National Ballet and Netherlands Opera regularly perform. The Royal Concertgebouw Orchestra, the Netherlands Philharmonic Orchestra and the Netherlands Chamber Orchestra are also based in the city. The old **Stadsschouwburg** on the Leidseplein hosts some of the world's top modern dance troupes, as well as offering excellent theatre productions with the odd English-language performance. There are several other venues where you can find dance, drama and music being performed, ranging from stalwart classics to the more cutting-edge.

Amsterdam is young and vibrant, and you'll find plenty of more modern and upbeat music around the city. Big-name bands will almost always perform in Amsterdam as part of their major European tours. The **Paradiso** (see page 105), the **Melkweg**

⬧ *Visit Rembrandt House Museum for an overview of the artist's life and work*

● *The Stadsschouwburg Theatre*

(see page 118) and the **Amsterdam ArenA** (see page 32) are three of the bigger venues, but in smaller halls and clubs throughout the city you'll find variations of rock, world music, folk, jazz and blues. Amsterdammers love music, and musicians seem to love the city in return.

If you are interested in history and the fine arts, there are plenty of small museums, churches and other old buildings of architectural interest to keep you occupied. But whatever you do, don't miss out on the things that really make Amsterdam stand out: Van Gogh, Rembrandt, the infamous red light district and cannabis culture, the brown bars, cafés, and its general ambience.

◗ *Bikes and canals are ubiquitous*

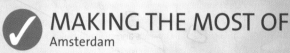

MAKING THE MOST OF
Amsterdam

Shopping

Thankfully, Amsterdam is not the neon-lit shopping capital of the world. As well as designer names and department stores, the city offers individual shops and boutiques selling anything from clogs to condoms, Dutch cheese to diamonds, and explosive liqueurs to non-alcoholic tipples. Many excellent specialist shops can be found along the *negen straatjes* (nine streets) running from the Singel canal to Prinsengracht.

If you're on the hunt for a diamond ring or other piece of jewellery, then you'll find prices competitive and the selection impressive. You can also take a free factory tour to learn a bit about what you're buying (see pages 80 and 94).

○ *It's not just Edam and Gouda you'll find in Amsterdam*

USEFUL SHOPPING PHRASES

How much is...?
Hoeveel kost (het)...?
Hoo-fayl kost (het)...?

Can I try this on?
Mag ik dit passen?
Makh ik dit passen?

I'm a size...
Ik heb maat...
Ik hep maat...

I'll take this one
Deze neem ik
Day-ze naym ik

Other than jewellery shops, the best and certainly cheapest bargains are to be found in the flea markets, which take place around the city all week long. One of the biggest and best is held at Waterlooplein (see page 87) every day but Sunday. The Albert Cuypmarkt (see page 87) is also a colourful affair, with a few hundred stalls running between Ferdinand Bolstraat and Van Woustraat selling everything from cheap fashion and textiles to fresh vegetables. A visit to the Bloemenmarkt (Flower Market, see page 88) along the Singel canal near Muntplein will see you leaving with lots of colourful photos.

Foodies should head straight for the various busy food markets and in particular the cheese stalls. Everyone has heard of Edam and Gouda, but you'll quickly discover that these are actually two of the blandest cheeses made in the country. They're produced mainly for export – the Dutch keep the tastier cheeses for themselves. Spices, however, are anything but bland. Dutch links with Southeast Asia, especially Indonesia, mean that you'll find a variety of spices and unusual fruits on sale.

Eating & drinking

Amsterdam is buzzing with great places to eat, with everything from cheap cafés to the finest gourmet cuisine. Much on offer is international – there are excellent Italian, Japanese, Chinese, Indian, African, American and Caribbean restaurants – but traditional cuisine from the Netherlands and other countries close by, such as Belgium, Scandinavia and Germany, is also popular.

One international speciality you shouldn't miss is Indonesian food. There is a large Indonesian population in Amsterdam thanks to the close trading ties between the Netherlands and the former

BROWN BARS, COFFEESHOPS AND TASTING HOUSES

If you simply want a coffee, don't go to a coffeeshop, which is the term for shops that sell marijuana as well as the usual coffees, drinks and snacks. For the drug-free option, you need a café. If you're looking for a decent meal and not just a coffee, choose an *eetcafé*, which has a wider menu.

Brown bars and brown cafés are so-called because of their traditionally dark and smoky atmosphere – although nowadays smoking is only in designated sections or on the terrace. Brown bars serve more in the way of alcoholic drinks while brown cafés serve more soft; both offer food of some kind.

Look out for the remaining few *proeflokalen* (tasting houses). These were originally created for the distillers producing *jenever* (Dutch gin), though independent tasting houses soon sprang up too. There are still a few left around the city if you are looking for a drop of something stronger.

⬥ *Alfresco dining on Nieuwmarkt*

East Indies, and there are countless restaurants serving this tasty and spicy cooking. Try the *rijsttafel* (rice table), a selection of 12 or more beef, seafood and vegetable dishes served with rice. It can be extremely filling, so save it for when you're really hungry.

◔ Help the Amsterdammers get through some of that Heineken!

PRICE CATEGORIES

Ratings are based on the rough cost of a three-course meal
for one person, excluding drinks.

£ up to €20   ££ €20–30   £££ over €30

Indonesian restaurants are also good for non-meat dishes, although vegetarians should have no trouble in Amsterdam finding good food to eat. With the city's long association with alternative culture, vegetarianism has been around for many years. There are several dedicated vegetarian restaurants and most regular places offer meat-free options.

Hotel breakfasts are usually continental and included in the price of the room. If you want orange juice you may have to ask for it, as it isn't always served automatically. The Dutch tend to eat early, so lunch begins around noon and dinner is served from 18.00 onwards. Many restaurants start to wind down by 22.00, when last orders are taken. If you like to eat late, your choice will be somewhat limited and you should first check out opening hours.

Tipping is not a big part of Dutch culture. A service charge is usually included in the bill – simply round up to the nearest euro or leave any spare change if you have enjoyed particularly good service.

USEFUL DINING PHRASES
I'd like a table for (two) please
Graag een tafel voor (twee) personen
Khraakh an taa-fel for (tway) persoanen

Could I have the bill please?
De rekening alstublieft?
De ray-ken-ing als-too-bleeft?

Waiter!
Ober!
Oaber!

Does it have meat in it?
Zit er vlees in?
Zitt air flays in?

Where are the toilets?
Waar is het toilet?
Vaar is het twa-let?

Entertainment & nightlife

You'll find it hard not to have fun in Amsterdam. Whatever you want to do, you can usually do it here – and that includes a few things you can't do in too many other cities.

Amsterdam is beautiful by day but comes into its own after dark. The infamous red light district near Centraal Station might not be everyone's idea of a fun time, but it undeniably has its own kind of neon attraction and really shouldn't be missed.

The Leidseplein near the Jordaan district is where teenagers hang out in bars and cafés and is a lively place to go for fast food. A trendier area is Spuikwartier, around Spuistraat, packed with bars, clubs, restaurants and some of Amsterdam's best brown bars.

If Amsterdam is a party town any night of the year, it's double the fun when there's a festival going on. One of the biggest and best parties is the Queen's Day on 30 April, which sets the city's streets heaving. Throughout the year, particularly in summer, there are many music, theatre and film festivals.

For music, dance and drama performances of all sorts, Amsterdam can't be beaten. Weekly listings can be found in *Time Out* and on the excellent English language website ⓦ www.underwateramsterdam.com. Make sure you look for flyers in bars and music shops advertising local clubs and special gigs.

You can buy tickets for many events in tourist information offices and travel agents. Bigger hotels will also book tickets for you. Alternatively, one of the biggest ticket agencies in the city is **AUB Ticketshop** (ⓐ Leidseplein 26, terrace side ⓣ 020 795 9950 ⓦ www.amsterdamsuitburo.nl ⓛ 10.00–19.30 Mon–Fri, 10.00–18.00 Sat, 12.00–18.00 Sun ⓝ Tram: Leidseplein), whose website allows you to book tickets before you even leave home.

● *Celebrating Queen's Day on the water*

Cinemas often play big releases and American films in the original language, with Dutch subtitles. Children's films are often dubbed into Dutch; 'OV' means original version while 'NV' means it's dubbed.

Visitors looking for the gay and lesbian scene should have no trouble finding entertainment. Reguliersdwarsstraat, parallel to the Flower Market, is one hub featuring both gay and mixed clubs, bars and coffeeshops. Ask at the **COC Centre** (ⓐ Rozenstraat 14 ⓘ 020 626 3087 ⓦ www.cocamsterdam.nl ⓝ Tram: Rozengracht) for

⬤ *The elegant Magere Brug at night*

information on the gay scene. Or check out the **Pink Point of Presence** (ⓐ Corner of Raadhuisstraat and Keizersgracht ① 020 428 1070 ⓦ www.pinkpoint.org ⓛ 10.00–18.00 Ⓝ Tram: Westermarkt), located next to the Homomonument, the city's memorial to gays and lesbians targeted by the Nazis.

One word of warning for those letting their hair down: the city's tolerance may mean that soft drugs are openly smoked in some nightclubs, but be aware that the buying and selling of drugs is still technically illegal.

Sport & relaxation

SPECTATOR SPORTS
Football
City stars **AFC Ajax** (ⓦ www.ajax.nl), historically one of the world's most successful football clubs, play at the Amsterdam ArenA. Fans will want to take the stadium tour. ⓐ Arena Blvd 1 ⓣ 020 311 1333 ⓦ www.amsterdamarena.nl ⓜ Metro: Bijlmer ArenA

Ice hockey
If you want to catch a match, the Amstel Tijgers are the local amateur team. They play at the Jaap Edenhal. ⓐ Radioweg 64 ⓣ 020 694 9652 ⓦ www.jaapeden.nl ⓜ Tram: 9

PARTICIPATION SPORTS
Bicycle rental
With nearly half a million bikes and 400 km of cycle paths, Amsterdam and the bicycle were truly made for each other. To rent one, try **MacBike** (ⓐ Various locations including Waterlooplein, Leidseplein and Centraal Station ⓣ 020 620 0985 ⓦ www.macbike.nl) and remember to take your passport.

Cycle tours
Enjoy a guided cycle tour of the city or further afield. Try **Mike's Bike Tours** (ⓐ Kerkstraat 134 ⓣ 020 622 7970 ⓦ www.mikesbike toursamsterdam.com), **Yellow Bike Tours** (ⓐ Nieuwzijds Kolk 29 ⓣ 020 620 6940 ⓦ www.yellowbike.nl) or the more off-beat **Orange Bike** (ⓐ Gelderskade 37 or Singel 233 ⓣ 020 528 9990 ⓦ www.orangebike.nl). All three of these companies also offer bike rentals.

Rollerblading

Every Friday night thousands of skaters take a 14.5-km (9-mile) route through the city centre, before gathering in Vondelpark at 20.00 (20.15 in winter). ⓦ www.fridaynightskate.com

RELAXATION

Blijburg aan Zee

A man-made beach with restaurant, mixing exotic and hippy, where trendy locals drink, eat tapas and listen to DJs. ❸ Bert Haanstrakade 2004 ❶ 020 416 0330 ⓦ www.blijburg.nl ⓝ Tram: IJburg

Sauna

For some pampering, head for **Sauna Deco** (❷ Herengracht 115 ❶ 020 623 8215 ⓦ www.saunadeco.nl ⓛ 12.00–23.00 Mon & Wed–Sat, 15.00–23.00 Tues, 13.00–19.00 Sun ⓝ Tram: Dam). **Sauna Fenomeen** is a slightly cheaper choice (❸ Eerste Schinkelstraat 14 ❶ 020 671 6780 ⓦ www.saunafenomeen.nl ⓛ 13.00–23.00 daily ⓝ Bus: 62, 142, 170, 171, 172, 197, 370 ❶ Mondays are women-only).

● *Ajax fans in the Amsterdam ArenA*

Accommodation

Amsterdam has hotels of all types and all standards, scattered throughout the city.

If you're after a lively time and don't mind the noise, look for accommodation around Centraal Station and near to Dam Square. If you like somewhere quieter with more character, search out the Jordaan neighbourhood or around the Canal Ring. Some of the tall canal-side buildings have been converted into atmospheric hotels. Note that they often don't have a lift, so if you have trouble with stairs do check in advance. For an alternative experience you can also stay on the canals, as some boats have been turned into floating B&Bs. The Museum district is a peaceful area and handy for the museums, with many fine cafés and restaurants nearby as well as the Vondelpark. The city's attractions are easily reached on foot pretty much wherever you stay.

A continental breakfast is usually included in the price of a room.

HOTELS

Acacia £ Right by a canal in the Jordaan district. No lift. The friendly owners also rent out rooms in two nearby canal boats.
❸ Lindengracht 251 (Western Canal Ring) ❶ 020 622 1460
Ⓦ www.hotelacacia.nl Ⓝ Tram: Nieuwe Willemsstraat

PRICE CATEGORIES
Ratings are based on the average cost of a standard room for two people for one night.
£ up to €100   ££ €100–200   £££ over €200

> **BOOK EARLY**
> Amsterdam is a small, old city but a popular one, and there isn't really enough accommodation to deal with the huge numbers of visitors who flock here. Book well ahead, especially at weekends and in summer, and don't expect to find anything really cheap. Even in winter, when room rates drop and you can sometimes find special deals, you should still plan ahead. Turning up in Amsterdam without booking a room in advance is definitely not recommended.

Amstel Botel £ This floating hotel in the dock across the IJ from Centraal Station is a bargain for three-star comfort, though it can be a bit noisy. ⓐ NDSM Shipyard, Pier 3 (Central Amsterdam) ❶ 020 626 4247 ⓦ www.amstelbotel.nl ⓝ Tram/metro: Centraal Station

Bicycle Hotel Amsterdam £ Friendly, affordable hotel in a great neighbourhood. Offers bike rental. ⓐ Van Ostadestraat 123 (Eastern Canal Ring & Plantage) ❶ 020 679 3452 ⓦ www.bicyclehotel.com ⓝ Tram: Ceintuurbaan

Winston £ Arty and edgy but affordable, the Winston is located on Amsterdam's oldest street. Each hotel room has been designed by a different artist from around the world – everything from Gothic chambers to Polaroid wallpaper – which makes for plenty of unique experiences. The downstairs bar hosts trendy avant-garde performances and the red light district is on your doorstep. ⓐ Warmoesstraat 129 (Central Amsterdam) ❶ 020 623 1380 ⓦ www.winston.nl ⓝ Tram/metro: Centraal Station

Bridge Hotel ££ Right on the Amstel river where it crosses the Canal Ring, this hotel is slightly out of the centre in a quiet area. Good-sized comfortable rooms. ⓐ Amstel 107–111 (Central Amsterdam) ⓘ 020 623 7068 ⓦ www.thebridgehotel.nl ⓝ Tram/metro: Waterlooplein

Keizershof ££ A converted 1672 canal house with just four beamed rooms, though the authentic historical feel means that not all rooms are en-suite. Great character and breakfast. ⓐ Keizersgracht 618 (Central Amsterdam) ⓘ 020 622 2855 ⓦ www.hotelkeizershof.nl ⓝ Tram: Keizersgracht

Lloyd Hotel & Cultural Embassy ££ Located in the fashionable Docklands area just east of Centraal Station, Lloyd offers open spaces, harbour views and unconventional décor. Choose from one-star to five-star rooms (the designation based largely on amount of floor space), depending on your pocket or mood. ⓐ Oostelijke Handelskade 34 (Eastern Canal Ring & Plantage) ⓘ 020 561 3636 ⓦ www.lloydhotel.com ⓝ Tram: Rietlandpark

Seven Bridges ££ Near the Amstel river, with views of seven bridges, this old canal house has antique décor and makes for an affordable yet stylish stay. ⓐ Reguliersgracht 31 (Central Amsterdam) ⓘ 020 623 1329 ⓦ www.sevenbridgeshotel.nl ⓝ Tram: Keizersgracht or Rembrandtplein

Singel Hotel ££ Friendly hotel with a pleasant old-world atmosphere overlooking the Singel canal in a quiet location near Centraal Station. ⓐ Singel 13–17 (Central Amsterdam) ⓘ 020 626 3108 ⓦ www.singelhotel.nl ⓝ Tram/metro: Centraal Station

▲ A suite at the eclectic Lloyd Hotel & Cultural Embassy

The Dylan £££ This celebrity hang-out, until recently known as Blakes, is based around a 17th-century former theatre. It is set back from the canal front and decorated in a restrained modern style. ⓐ Keizersgracht 384 (Central Amsterdam) ⓣ 020 530 2010 ⓦ www.dylanamsterdam.com ⓝ Tram: Keizersgracht or Leidseplein

Hotel Pulitzer £££ Perhaps the best treat in Amsterdam for a splurge or a romantic weekend, the Pulitzer comprises a maze of old canal houses that are now the ultimate in modern comfort. Highly recommended. ⓐ Prinsengracht 315–331 (Western Canal Ring) ⓣ 020 523 5235 ⓦ www.pulitzeramsterdam.com ⓝ Tram: Westermarkt

⬤ *Amsterdam's beautiful Hotel Pulitzer*

APARTMENTS

Amsterdam House £ This company has several canal-side apartments you can rent by the week plus ten houseboats. Live right among the houseboat-dwellers of Amsterdam for less than it costs to stay in a hotel. ⓐ Office: 's-Gravelandseveer 7 (Central Amsterdam) ① 020 626 2577 ⓦ www.amsterdamhouse.com ⓝ Tram: Spui or Muntplein

Maes B&B ££ Named after famous Dutch painter Nicolaes Maes, this is one of the city's oldest B&Bs and is known for its pleasant ambience. Very comfortable, with numerous staircases leading to attractive rooms with big bathrooms. Apartments also available. ⓐ Herenstraat 26 (Western Canal Ring) ① 020 427 5165 ⓦ www.bedandbreakfastamsterdam.com ⓝ Tram/metro: Centraal Station or Nieuwezijds Kolk

HOSTELS & CAMPSITES

Camping Het Amsterdamse Bos £ This campsite is fairly far from the city centre but has cabins to rent – great since Amsterdam can be wet. ⓐ Kliene Noorddijk 1, Amstelveen ① 020 641 6868 ⓦ www.campingamsterdamsebos.nl ⓝ Tram: Amstelveen Binnenhof, then bus: 171

NJHC City Hostel Vondelpark £ Part of the Hostelling International group, this hostel is south of the Vondelpark and is handy for both the Museum district and the city centre. ⓐ Zandpad 5 (Museumplein) ① 020 589 8996 ⓝ Tram: Leidseplein or Overtoom

Vliegenbos campsite £ One of the closest campsites to the city centre. ⓐ Meeuwenlaan 138 ① 020 636 8855 ⓛ Apr–end Sept ⓝ Bus: 32, 33, 361. Stop is 200 m (219 yds) from campsite

THE BEST OF AMSTERDAM

You'll enjoy Amsterdam no matter how short or long a visit you have. Whether you're after culture, nightlife or the relaxed atmosphere, if time is tight decide on your priorities and don't try to squeeze in too much.

TOP 10 ATTRACTIONS

- **Amsterdams Historisch Museum** A lively exploration of the fascinating history of this unique city (see page 66).

- **Anne Frank House** This museum and house is an essential (and moving) stop for a first-time visitor to the city (see page 106).

- **Begijnhof** An amazing historical old square – home to the city's oldest house – that survives in the heart of Amsterdam (see page 60).

- **Dam Square** This huge square at the hub of city life is not especially picturesque, but its historical interest cannot be questioned (see page 62).

Traditional wooden clogs from Amsterdam

- **Jordaan district** Once an overcrowded working-class slum, this is now one of the prettiest quarters of the city, relaxing but fun and great for photography (see page 110).

- **Museum Amstelkring** A fascinating historical museum in the heart of the red light district with a once-secret Catholic church at the top (see page 68).

- **De Oude Kerk (The Old Church)** The oldest building in Amsterdam, with stained glass windows from the 1550s, and the finest of the city's several old churches (see page 70).

- **Museum Het Rembrandthuis** The home and studio of one of the city's artistic geniuses. Both ordinary and extraordinary at the same time (see page 69).

- **Rijksmuseum** The grandest of Amsterdam's two most popular art museums, with an unrivalled collection that includes portraits by Dutch masters Rembrandt and Vermeer (see page 96).

- **Van Gogh Museum** People travel from around the world to see this, the finest collection of Van Gogh's work all housed in one place and much else besides (see page 98).

Suggested itineraries

HALF-DAY: AMSTERDAM IN A HURRY

If you only have a few hours, forget the big museums; you'll never do them justice. Instead, walk through the red light district (see page 67) and visit Amsterdam's oldest monument, De Oude Kerk (see page 70), and Zuider Kerk, a 17th-century church near Waterlooplein. Continue on to the Museum Het Rembrandthuis (see page 69), which can be visited quickly. Then make your way to the Herengracht canal and look for a canal-side café or restaurant.

1 DAY: TIME TO SEE A LITTLE MORE

Start early and beat the crowds at the Rijksmuseum (see page 96) or the Van Gogh Museum (see page 98). Then visit Museum Het Rembrandthuis and the red light district, take in Dam Square (see page 62) and head west across four canals to reach the Jordaan district (see page 110). You'll find plenty of shopping opportunities along with bars and cafés, plus a terrific choice of eating places for an atmospheric evening meal.

2–3 DAYS: TIME TO SEE MUCH MORE

You can take in both of the major museums and more of the Top 10 Attractions (see pages 40–41), including the Anne Frank House (see page 106). Take time to relax by visiting the Vondelpark (see page 95) or the Plantage (see page 78), with its museums, planetarium and zoo.

LONGER: ENJOYING AMSTERDAM TO THE FULL

With more time at your disposal, you will have time to make use of the good train network and take a train to Rotterdam (see page 130) or The Hague (see page 120) to see another side of Dutch life. You can see more of the 'real' Amsterdam, too, outside of the centre, including the fascinating multicultural district of De Pijp. Start each day with one of the major sights: Rijksmuseum, Van Gogh Museum and Anne Frank House. Get there 15 minutes before opening time to avoid the queues.

⬥ *Busy Dam Square is at the heart of the city*

Something for nothing

If you're looking to enjoy Amsterdam without spending too much money, you'll find plenty to do. Some of the top sights in the city are free, such as the Begijnhof (see page 60), the Bloemenmarkt (Flower Market, see page 88) and the hidden treat that is the **Hollandsche Manege** (Dutch Riding School ❷ Vondelstraat 140 ❶ 020 618 0942 ❼ www.dehollandschemanege.nl ❶ 09.30–22.00 Mon–Fri, 09.30–18.00 Sat & Sun ❼ Tram: Overtoom).

If you love music, culture and partying, the best way to enjoy the city inexpensively is to visit during one of its many festivals. Try the Amsterdam Roots Festival on the third Sunday in June, or check out free open-air theatre in the Vondelpark from June to August. The Uitmarkt is a season of culture with music and theatre performances taking place all over town. Be prepared for large crowds.

If you're a bargain-hunting museum lover, you should come during the second weekend in April for National Museum Weekend. Entry to the city's museums over the weekend is free, although you'll have to struggle through the crowds.

At other times it's a good idea to buy the **I amsterdam Card** (❼ www.iamsterdam.com) from a tourist office, which combines a public transport ticket with discounted entry to many museums and other attractions.

The canal-side paths make for beautiful strolls and there is always a cheap and cheerful café or bar in which to take a break. Street markets are an endless source of free fun and good photographs. You can put together a picnic at the food markets and take it to one of the city's many parks to stroll, relax and eat. Head to a street stall for some cheap, filling snacks, including the Dutch favourite: herring.

Rollerbladers can join the free Friday Night Skate (see page 33), which starts at the Vondelpark at about 20.00 for a two-hour tour of the city.

Finally, there is always the red light district. It's a source of endless fascination for visitors ... and it costs nothing to look.

🔺 *Stop for the obligatory photo on the Magere Brug*

When it rains

It rains a fair bit in Amsterdam. Wet weather is not a problem, though, because the city is used to it. You can still take a trip in a canal boat, for instance, just under cover. You can also enjoy a visit to the Hortus Botanicus (Botanical Gardens, see page 80), which has some great indoor greenhouses and a wonderful butterfly house.

In fact, rain is a good opportunity to linger in the main museums and really admire Rembrandt, Vermeer and Van Gogh's work. When the sun is shining outside, you might be tempted to whizz by the paintings and end up missing a lot. You can also take the time to visit Amsterdam's countless smaller museums and churches, which are more quietly spectacular. The modern science museum NEMO (see page 65), will keep you busy for hours.

Wet weather is part of the Dutch lifestyle and looked on as an opportunity to relax. You can join in with the locals by spending longer in the bars and cafés, chatting and taking it easy. The people are friendly and open, so striking up conversations is never difficult. Make the effort and you'll get an insight into the city that most visitors miss because they're too busy rushing around all the sights. The best area to do this is the Jordaan (see page 110), a quiet residential district near the heart of the city. Although popular with visitors, you'll also meet plenty of locals in its wide choice of bars, cafés and restaurants.

Alternatively, make it a shopping day and head to a department store or covered shopping centre, such as at Schiphol Airport or the more upmarket Magna Plaza, located directly behind the Koninklijk Paleis in the beautiful former main post office.

If the rain looks steady for the day, check to see if the weather's better in Rotterdam or The Hague and jump on a train heading south.

🔺 Stay out of the rain in a covered canal boat

On arrival

TIME DIFFERENCE

Amsterdam is on Central European Time (CET), one hour ahead of London. Daylight saving applies. Clocks go forward one hour at the end of March and fall back one hour at the end of October.

ARRIVING

By air

Schiphol Airport (ⓐ Evert van de Beekstraat 202 ❶ 020 601 9111 ⓦ www.schiphol.nl) is 18 km (11 miles) southwest of the city centre and has one terminal and various wings containing the usual amenities, including ATMs, shops, car hire, ample seating areas, restaurants, as well as a public shopping plaza connected to a bustling train station. It also has a small art museum just after passport control and a casino to while away the hours.

⬤ *Schiphol Airport is a major international hub*

If you haven't booked a hotel, try Booking.com's reservation desk, or the tourist information office located in arrivals lounge 2.

The airport is linked to the city centre by regular trains, which take about 15 minutes to reach Centraal Station. There are usually seven trains every hour during the day and about one an hour during the night. Buy your ticket (€3.80 one-way) from a counter near the station entrance before boarding the train. KLM sometimes offers passengers a free train journey to Centraal Station as part of the airfare; ask when booking.

The Interliner 370 bus costs about the same as the train but takes slightly longer. It will leave you at the Leidseplein. Some hotels run transfer buses from the airport.

Taxis also take longer than trains to reach the city centre and cost several times as much. Unless you have a huge amount of luggage it is probably preferable to get a train to Centraal Station, and take a taxi from there to your accommodation.

By rail

The main station, **Amsterdam Centraal** (Centraal Station) lies at the centre of the city's loop of canals, with its back to the IJ waterfront. Most trains, both national and international, start or finish here.

All trains within the Netherlands are operated by the **Nederlandse Spoorwegen** or NS, which means Dutch Railways (W www.ns.nl). To avoid long queues, try the ticket machines around the station, which offer an English-language option but often don't accept foreign credit or debit cards. There are also regular ticket booths. Most international tickets must be bought at the booths, which are located at the entrance to the western hall of the station. Be sure to buy a ticket, regardless of your destination. They cannot be bought on board and you face an immediate fine of around €60 if caught without one.

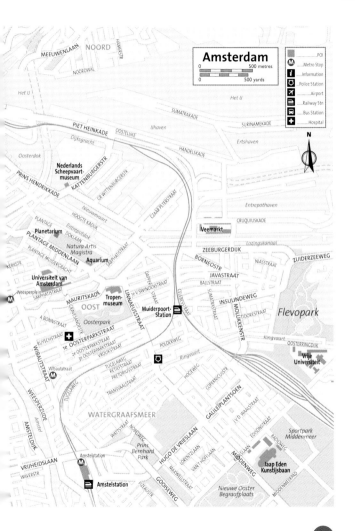

Centraal Station is undergoing long-term construction works for the new north–south metro line, so allow plenty of time. The station has the usual facilities, including metro links and a tourist office on platform 2B. **Lost property** (➌ Stationsplein 15 ➊ 020 557 8544) keeps items for five days before shipping them to Utrecht. You'll need ID to reclaim anything.

By road

Amsterdam's most central terminus for its bus and tram network is directly outside Centraal Station. The city's public transport service **GVB** (➊ 020 460 6060 ➐ www.gvb.nl) has an office here for maps, information, and either single tickets or the new OV-*chipkaart* (public transport card), which works much like the Oyster card in London. Another useful transport planning site is ➐ www.ov9292.nl

Regional buses are operated by **Connexxion** (➊ 0900 266 6399 ➐ www.connexxion.nl) and **Arriva** (➊ 0900 202 2022 ➐ www.arriva.nl). The regional bus station is on Marnixstraat, which is fairly central.

International Eurolines coaches arrive at Amstel Station, which is linked to the city centre by train as well as by metro lines 51, 53 and 54 and by tram line 12.

Driving in Amsterdam is not recommended: crowded, narrow streets, looping concentric canals and one-way systems traversing this already compact city guarantee regular traffic jams. Parking in the centre is both difficult and expensive, with most parking spaces having metres that need to be fed hourly, or limited parking times. There are car parks at Prins Hendrikkade 20A, Valkenburgerstraat 238, Tesselschadestraat 1G and Van Baerlestraat 33B, but you may be better off using the Park & Ride system at Bijlmer ArenA, Bos en Lommer, Olympic Stadium, Sloterdijk and Zeeburg stations.

FINDING YOUR FEET

Amsterdam is a traveller-friendly city. Almost everyone speaks English and people are willing to give directions if you need them. It is generally pleasant and safe to wander around, but do take special care around Centraal Station, which attracts pickpockets and petty thieves. Likewise, keep an eye on your bag in the red light district.

In particular, beware of cyclists. They do pedal fast and because many junctions along the canals are four-way it is important to look in every direction. Keep an eye out for the trams, too.

ORIENTATION

The city centre can seem confusing at first, as one *gracht*, or canal, looks much like another. The way that several canals circle the city centre in a horseshoe shape also means you might get easily confused about which direction you're facing. That said, many of the sights can be found on or near a canal and walking along one until you reach your destination is an excellent and pleasant way of getting to know the city.

IF YOU GET LOST, TRY …

Do you speak English?
Spreekt u Engels?
Spraykt-oo Eng-els?

Is this the way to...?
Is dit de weg naar...?
Is dit de vekh naar...?

Could you point it out on the map?
Kunt u het op de kaart aanwijzen?
Kunt oo het op de kaart aan-wayezen?

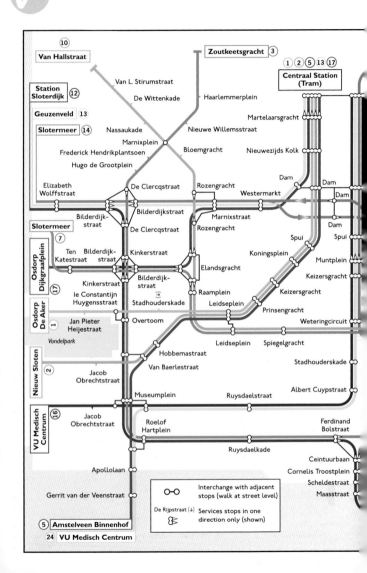

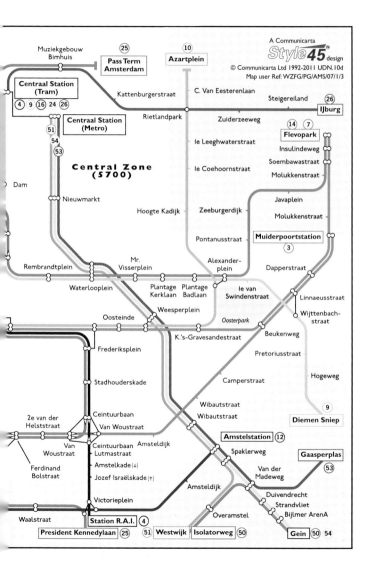

MONEY-SAVING TRAVEL

The best way to save money on public transport is to buy the OV-*chipkaart*, a smartcard with a chip onto which you can load credit, much like the Oyster card in London. It can be bought at vending machines in the station. You can also buy disposable cards, but these cannot be topped up. Swipe the card as you enter and leave the station and you will automatically be charged for the distance travelled. The same card works in other cities in the Netherlands. See Ⓦ www.ov-chipkaart.nl

Don't rush into buying, though, until you know where you are staying and how close you are to the attractions you want to see. If the weather's fine, then Amsterdam is an easy and pleasant city to walk around.

The four main canals radiate out from the centre in the following order: Singel, Herengracht, Keizersgracht and Prinsengracht. There are hundreds of bridges and smaller canals connecting the larger ones – the good news is that getting lost is great fun.

Centraal Station is located in the middle of the city's U-shaped canals at the mouth of the IJ waterfront. If you head south along Damrak you'll come to Dam Square, a major meeting point. Carry on down Rokin then turn right around the Koningsplein (flower market) and then straight down Leidsestraat to reach the touristy Leidseplein. This square is slightly above the Vondelpark, the biggest park in the city.

The red light district is a five-minute walk from the station, in the area just north of Dam Square, while the Jordaan district lies to the west. Beyond the canal ring encircling the city is the Museumplein, or Museum district.

It's worth getting a detailed map as many of the best finds are on smaller streets. Several of the tobacconists near Leidseplein sell city maps, or you can print out maps to specific locations from the machine next to the ticket office in Centraal Station.

GETTING AROUND

You can cross Amsterdam's central canal hub on foot in about an hour and walking is a pleasant way of getting around.

In terms of regular public transport, the tram is the easiest and the most popular option. The tram network covers the city centre, with 15 lines running regularly until 00.15. When travelling on most lines you must buy your tickets in advance and validate them on the tram, or buy an OV-*chipkaart* (see opposite). Some newer trams have been introduced with conductors on board; on these you must enter through the rear doors and either show the conductor your ticket, or buy one on board.

There's a metro within the city centre, but it is used mainly to serve the suburbs. Three lines (51, 53 and 54) travel between Centraal Station, Nieuwmarkt and Waterlooplein, the city-centre stops most likely to interest visitors. A new line should be open by 2017.

Buses are more useful for venturing further afield, although there are some city-centre bus routes too. Night buses in the centre run from 24.00 to 07.00, along routes that connect to Centraal Station, Rembrandtplein and Leidseplein. There is also a small bus that follows a circular route around the Prinsengracht to the Oosterdok. It is called the Stop/Go and can be boarded anywhere along the route, including Centraal Station. See Ⓦ www.gvb.nl

It is a good idea to pick up a free *English-language Tourist Guide to Public Transport* from any tourist office when you first arrive. It explains everything you need to know.

MUSEUM BOAT

It makes a pleasant change to travel across the city on the canals using the Amsterdam Museum Boat. The boat operates all day and you can hop on or off as many times as you like. There are stops at attractions such as the Stopera, Rijksmuseum, Anne Frank House, Nederlands Scheepvaart Museum (Maritime Museum) as well as Centraal Station. Tickets also include a reduction of up to 50 per cent on museum entrance fees.

Taxis are best picked up at taxi ranks on major road junctions and outside the main hotels. You can flag one down in the street if it is empty. Common practice for tipping is to round the fare up to the nearest convenient amount.

Car hire

There is no need to hire a car if you plan to stay in the city. If you want a car for exploring further afield, the easiest place to rent one is Schiphol Airport. Agencies based there include Avis, Budget, Hertz, National Car Rental and Sixt. In the centre, try:

Alamo ⓐ Overtoom 197 ⓣ 020 683 2123 ⓦ www.alamo.com

Avis ⓐ Nassaukade 380 ⓣ 020 683 6061 ⓦ www.avis.nl

Hertz ⓐ Overtoom 333 ⓣ 020 612 2441 ⓦ www.hertz.com

Tiger ⓦ www.tigercarrental.com

ⓞ *Traditional merchants' houses line the canals*

 THE CITY OF
Amsterdam

Central Amsterdam

Central Amsterdam, sometimes called the old town or the medieval quarter, is the heart of the city. Here you'll find the main railway station, the main square, several museums, old churches and the infamous red light district. Several of the major sights in the city are located in the area, in particular the unmissable Museum Het Rembrandthuis.

As well as the inevitable modern buildings, hotels, restaurants and shops you'll come across lovely traditional churches and narrow gabled buildings in the side streets. Amsterdam is an old but vibrant city, where traditional and modern styles thrive together. De Oude Kerk, for example, the oldest building in Amsterdam, sits right in the heart of the brash, neon-lit red light district.

SIGHTS & ATTRACTIONS

Amsterdam Centraal (Centraal Station)

As well as being a major transport hub, Amsterdam Centraal is an attraction in its own right as a fine example of late 19th-century architecture. It was designed by Petrus Josephus Hubertus Cuypers, the architect who also built the Rijksmuseum. Built on three specially created artificial islands and resting on 30,000 pylons, the station was originally a source of controversy as it separated the city from the river for the first time. But like many controversial buildings, time has allowed it to win over the hearts of the local people. ❸ Stationsplein ❶ 020 557 8400 ⓥ Tram/metro: Centraal Station

Begijnhof

This square is not only an amazing, quiet oasis right in the middle of the bustle of Amsterdam, but contains the oldest house in the

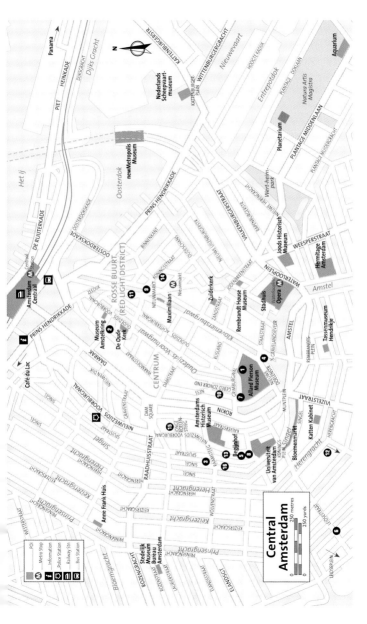

Central Amsterdam

0   250 metres
0   250 yards

city. To find it, take the narrow, gated alleyway on the north side of Spui, at No 14. Alternatively, until 17.00, you can reach it from the Amsterdams Historisch Museum (see feature box on page 66).

The square has been here since 1346, when it was used as part of a convent for the Beguines. Theirs was a more liberal order than most, as the nuns did not have to take the usual vows of poverty, chastity and obedience and were allowed to own property while also doing their good work for the poor and the sick. The original buildings have gone, but the garden and courtyard are still surrounded by some of Amsterdam's finest and oldest buildings.

No 34 is Het Houten Huis (The Wooden House), which dates back to about 1470 or earlier and is one of the most photographed sights in the city. No 30 conceals a secret chapel, built in 1671, which can be visited.

There are no nuns here these days. The last member of the order to live here died in 1971; the grand houses are now rented out to female students and elderly women. ⓐ Gedempte Begijnensloot, off Spui ⓦ www.begijnhofamsterdam.nl ⓛ Square & chapel: 13.00–18.30 Mon, 09.00–18.30 Tues–Fri, 09.00–18.00 Sat & Sun ⓝ Tram: Spui

Dam Square

Dam Square, known simply as the Dam, is the location of the original 13th-century dam across the Amstel river that gives the city its name. The square, once a large fish market, has gradually became the hub of city life. While no one can pretend it is one of the most picturesque squares in the world, it is a great spot for people-watching. Take care crossing the large square as tourists, locals, bikes and vehicles of all kinds come at you from several directions.

⬤ Centraal Station is a fine building in its own right

Look out for the massive Koninklijk Paleis (Royal Palace) dominating the west end of the square. It looks more like a civic building than a royal residence, which it is in part. The palace is occasionally open for tours, but the days and times are erratic.

Near the palace stands the Nieuwe Kerk (New Church). The name is misleading. The church dates from the 16th century and therefore is only new in relation to the Oude Kerk (Old Church). It hosts many international art exhibitions and often collaborates with St Petersburg's world famous State Hermitage Museum.

Also in Dam Square, at the far end from the church and palace, is the Nationaal Monument, commemorating the citizens of Amsterdam who suffered during the Nazi occupation of World War II. ⊙ Tram: Dam

newMetropolis Museum (NEMO)

There's no mistaking the newMetropolis Museum, or NEMO. It looks uncannily like a giant ship, or even a green spaceship, as you approach it from the bridge across the Oosterdok southeast of Centraal Station. The controversial structure was designed by Renzo Piano and is worth a visit even if only to see the view over Amsterdam from its roof.

NEMO is a science and technology centre with three floors of interactive exhibits. You can learn anything from how light and sound waves work, to how cheese is made, to how to perform a surgical operation. This place is fun for kids of all ages.

🔻 *The striking newMetropolis Museum (NEMO)*

ⓐ Oosterdok 2 ❶ 020 531 3233 Ⓦ www.e-nemo.nl ❶ 10.00–17.00
Tues–Sun (Sept–May); 10.00–17.00 (June–Aug & school holidays)
Ⓝ Tram/metro: Centraal Station ❶ Admission charge

HISTORY LESSON

Amsterdam's fascinating history of ships and the sea, of
spices, diamonds and – more recently – sex, drugs and rock
and roll, is explored in its excellent **Amsterdams Historisch
Museum (Historical Museum)**. It's a great place to visit at the
start of a visit to the city.

The building itself is part of Amsterdam's history. A convent
in the 16th century, it later became an orphanage. The
museum is still divided into two by the trench that once
separated boys from girls.

Follow the galleries and you see how Amsterdam developed
from being a tiny fishing village at the start of the 13th century
through to its heyday in the 17th century. It was the damming of
the Amstel river, originally done to reduce flooding, which led to
this development; ships were forced to unload their cargoes
here, creating jobs and making the town a trading centre.

The city's unique artistic and cultural movements arose
from the expansion of its trade and industry, and the recent
influx of foreign workers. The museum follows the city's history
right through to the present day and gives you a good idea of
what makes Amsterdam tick. ⓐ Kalverstraat 92, Nieuwezijds
Voorburgwal 357, Sint Luciënsteeg 27 ❶ 020 523 1822
Ⓦ www.ahm.nl ❶ 10.00–17.00 Mon–Fri, 11.00–17.00 Sat, Sun
& holidays Ⓝ Tram: Spui or Muntplein ❶ Admission charge

Rosse Buurt/De Wallen (Red light district)

The red light district is usually the one area of a city most visitors avoid. In Amsterdam it's the opposite; the place is filled not only with prostitutes and live sex shows but with tourists who come simply to stand and stare. The girls sit openly in the windows of little apartments, dressed or, more accurately, undressed, in a range of outrageous and skimpy outfits. It is not a place to go if you are easily shocked.

The area itself would be quite a picturesque part of Amsterdam, with its narrow canal-side streets, but it is not a good idea to get your camera out. The girls, and their protectors in the streets outside, don't take kindly to having their picture taken. The city has recently embarked on a clean-up of the area, closing some of the windows and renting out various buildings to upmarket shops and boutiques. The police keep the district fairly safe for visitors, but do watch out for pickpockets and avoid any dodgy-looking behaviour.

ⓐ Roughly south of Zeedijk, north of Damstraat and east of Damrak
ⓝ Tram: Dam; metro: Nieuwmarkt

Tassenmuseum Hendrikje (Museum of Bags & Purses)

An unusual museum showcasing women's handbags and purses throughout Western history, this is a bit like walking into a film star's wardrobe. The collection encompasses around 3,500 bags, pouches, suitcases and the like, from medieval times to contemporary designs. It offers an insight into the bag's function as well as the variety of shapes and materials used to make them. Even better, the museum shop offers a large array of bags by contemporary Dutch and foreign designers. It is hard to resist buying one after being taunted by so many fashionable examples.

ⓐ Herengracht 573 ⓣ 020 524 6452 ⓦ www.tassenmuseum.nl
ⓛ 10.00–17.00 ⓝ Tram/metro: Waterlooplein ⓘ Admission charge

Zuiderkerk

Near the Rembrandt House Museum (see opposite) is the Zuiderkerk, a grand Gothic construction built in 1611. Its high tower is open in summer for those who can manage all the steps and has great views. The tower entrance is outside the church, which is now the Amsterdam council's information and display centre. ⓐ Zandstraat ⓣ 020 689 2565 ⓛ Church: 12.00–17.00 Mon–Fri; tower tours every 30 mins 12.00–16.00 Mon–Sat (Apr–Sept) ⓜ Tram/metro: Waterlooplein ⓘ Admission charge for tower

CULTURE

Katten Kabinet

The death of his favourite cat sparked the founder of the Katten Kabinet to open what is probably the world's only museum featuring an art collection focused solely on cats. Even allergic feline lovers can visit, as the cats here are painted ones. There is, however, more to see than just fur. The museum is located in a building dating back to 1667, which once housed Amsterdam's mayor and welcomed visitors such as American President John Adams. You can see its original ballroom and music chambers. ⓐ Herengracht 497 ⓣ 020 626 5378 ⓦ www.kattenkabinet.nl ⓛ 10.00–14.00 Mon–Fri, 12.00–17.00 Sat & Sun ⓜ Tram: Keizersgracht ⓘ Admission charge

Museum Amstelkring

One of the most fascinating museums in the city is the Amstelkring, housed in a 17th-century merchant's house in the heart of the red light district. Its location makes it all the more surprising that hidden in the upper floors is a complete Catholic church, built at a time when Catholics needed to be careful in Protestant Amsterdam.

Shoe-horned into this small space, there is no evidence of a church visible from outside – a condition of its existence, as Catholics were allowed to hold services in private buildings provided nothing outside indicated their presence. There were several such churches in Amsterdam, but this is the only one to survive in its original state.

The lower three floors of the museum are given over to displays of what life was like in a merchant's house such as this one, which was built, complete with church, in 1663. The church is currently closed for restoration till 2012, but the museum remains open. ⓐ Oudezijds Voorburgwal 40 ⓣ 020 624 6604 ⓦ www.museumamstelkring.nl ⓛ 10.00–17.00 Mon–Sat, 13.00–17.00 Sun & public holidays ⓝ Tram/metro: Centraal Station ⓘ Admission charge

Museum Het Rembrandthuis (Rembrandt House Museum)

To see a Rembrandt painting in the Rijksmuseum is one thing, but to visit his actual house and see the studio where he worked is quite another. The artist bought the house in 1639 and lived there for just over 20 years at the peak of his fame. He spent so much money furnishing the house, however, that he was eventually declared bankrupt and had to move to a more modest home in Jordaan, a working-class neighbourhood at the time.

It is fascinating to see the kitchen and, of course, the studio where Rembrandt worked. There's also a room displaying objects that he collected and studied: sculptures, stones, feathers and anything that interested him for its shape, texture or colour. There is a collection of the artist's work in a separate annexe, though this consists mostly of sketches. For his best works you need to visit the Rijksmuseum (see page 96).

The building is a fine, three-storey affair, but it can get crowded as some of the rooms are fairly small. Go early or late in the day if you can.

Jodenbreestraat 4–6 ⏱ 020 520 0400 🌐 www.rembrandthuis.nl
🕐 10.00–17.00 Ⓜ Tram/metro: Waterlooplein ⓘ Admission charge

De Oude Kerk (The Old Church)

If you only see one church in Amsterdam make it this one, the Old Church in the heart of the red light district. There's been a church on this spot since the mid-13th century, although the present building dates back to the mid-14th century. The highlights of the church are its wonderful stained-glass windows, some of which date back as far

🔺 *The historic spire of De Oude Kerk*

as the 1550s. When the light is bright they are stunningly beautiful, a complete contrast to the neon in the surrounding streets.

The church's interior these days is used for art displays and other shows and it is a venue for regular music concerts. Look for notices advertising the concerts and try to go, as it's quite an experience to sit and enjoy music here. ⓐ Oudekerksplein 23, off Oudezijds Voorburgwal ⓣ 020 625 8284 ⓦ www.oudekerk.nl ⓛ 11.00–17.00 Mon–Sat, 13.00–17.00 Sun ⓜ Tram: Dam; metro: Nieuwmarkt

RETAIL THERAPY

The centre of Amsterdam has all the shops typical of any major city, plus a few specialist shops you'd be hard pushed to find anywhere else.

Amsterdam Diamond Center The biggest diamond shop in the centre of the city, it also sells other jewellery and conventional souvenirs. Take a diamond tour before buying. ⓐ Rokin 1–5 ⓣ 020 624 5787 ⓦ www.amsterdamdiamondcenter.nl ⓛ 10.00–18.00 Mon–Sat (until 20.30 Thur), 11.00–18.00 Sun

De Bijenkorf Probably the most famous department store in the Netherlands; you'll realise why it's called 'The Beehive' if you visit. ⓐ Dam 1 ⓣ 09 000 919 (Netherlands only) ⓦ www.debijenkorf.nl ⓛ 11.00–19.00 Mon, 09.30–19.00 Tues, Wed, Fri & Sat, 09.30–21.00 Thur, 12.00–18.00 Sun

Condomerie Legendary condom specialists; see it to believe it. ⓐ Warmoesstraat 141 ⓣ 020 627 4174 ⓦ www.condomerie.com ⓛ 11.00–18.00 Mon–Sat ⓜ Tram: Dam; metro: Nieuwmarkt

Magna Plaza Amsterdam's first shopping centre, incorporated
into the city's old post office. ⓐ Nieuwezijds Voorburgwal 182
ⓦ www.magnaplaza.nl ⓛ 11.00–19.00 Mon, 10.00–19.00 Tues,
Wed, Fri & Sat, 10.00–21.00 Thur, 12.00–19.00 Sun ⓝ Tram: Dam

When Nature Calls This upmarket boutique sells legal herbal
concoctions that allegedly have similar effects to those of their
illegal cousins: pick up herbal ecstasy, energisers, hangover
cures and cannabis seeds for home-growers. These products
are not legal in every country, so don't travel abroad with them.
Mushrooms were banned in 2008. ⓐ Keizersgracht 508
ⓣ 020 330 0700 ⓦ www.whennaturecalls.nl ⓛ 10.00–22.00 daily
ⓝ Tram: Keizersgracht

TAKING A BREAK

You'll find plenty of choices in the city centre and more fast-food
places here than anywhere else in Amsterdam. Try Rokin, the major
street between Dam Square and Muntplein, Leidsestraat, which
leads from Leidseplein to Koningsplein, and the bustling
Nieuwmarkt square.

Atrium £ ❶ This café-cum-restaurant for staff and students at the
University of Amsterdam is also open to anyone wanting a cheap
meal in the city centre, and has a typically lively college atmosphere.
ⓐ Oudezijds Achterburgwal 237 ⓣ 020 525 3999 ⓛ 12.00–14.00,
17.00–19.00 Mon–Fri ⓝ Tram: Spui

De Bakkerswinkel £ ❷ Always bustling and crowded, this tea
room at the edge of the red light district is hectic but charming.

🚊 Warmoesstraat 69 📞 020 489 8000 🌐 www.debakkerswinkel.com
🕐 08.00–17.30 Tues–Fri, 09.00–18.00 Sat–Sun 🚋 Tram: Spui

Café Gollem £ ❸ One of the city's colourful brown cafés with an especially good collection of beers. 🚊 Raamsteeg 4 📞 020 626 6645 🌐 www.cafegollem.nl 🕐 16.00–01.00 Mon–Fri, 14.00–02.00 Sat & Sun 🚋 Tram: Spui

Café de Jaren £ ❹ Fine example of a grand café. Overlooking the Amstel, it manages to be both arty and down to earth at the same time. 🚊 Nieuwe Doelenstraat 20 📞 020 625 5771 🌐 www.cafedejaren.nl 🕐 09.30–01.00 Sun–Thur, 09.30–02.00 Fri & Sat 🚋 Tram: Spui or Muntplein

Hoppe £ ❺ This is another of the city's great brown cafés. It dates back to 1670 and the 17th-century atmosphere remains. While their main purpose seems to be to serve alcohol, you can also get a simple snack here. 🚊 Spuistraat 18–20 📞 020 420 4420 🌐 www.cafehoppe.com 🕐 07.30–01.00 Sun–Thur, 07.30–02.00 Fri & Sat 🚋 Tram: Spui

Maoz £ ❻ Amsterdam is the place to find falafel and Maoz is the place to eat it. This spankingly clean chain restaurant is cheap and the staff are exceedingly cheerful. 🚊 Leidsestraat 85 📞 020 625 0717 🕐 11.00–23.00 daily 🚋 Tram: Leidseplein

Pannenkoekenhuis £ ❼ Located up a steep staircase, this tiny restaurant serving traditional Dutch cuisine is a real time warp. Reservations recommended. 🚊 Grimburgwal 2 🕐 12.00–19.00 Mon–Fri, 12.00–18.00 Sat, 12.00–17.00 Sun 🚋 Tram: Muntplein

Café Luxembourg £–££ ❽ An excellent meeting place, lunch stop or coffee/beer break, this grand café with a terrace overlooking Spui Square is one of the city's places to see and be seen in. ⓐ Spuistraat 24 ① 020 620 6264 ⓦ www.luxembourg.nl ① 09.00–24.00 Mon–Thur, 09.00–01.00 Fri–Sun ⓝ Tram: Spui

In de Waag £–££ ❾ Worth a visit in its own right, this former guild house was home to one of the first anatomical theatres in Europe. As well as the café, it boasts some of the city's top innovative IT projects. ⓐ Nieuwmarkt 4 ① 020 422 7772 ⓦ www.indewaag.nl ① 09.00–22.30 daily ⓝ Metro: Nieuwmarkt

AFTER DARK

RESTAURANTS

Kapitein Zeppos £ ❿ An excellent venue serving Flemish and French cuisine, Zeppos is hidden away down a narrow, cobbled alley. Live music on Sundays. ⓐ Gebed Zonder End 5 ① 020 624 2057 ⓦ www.zeppos.nl ① 12.00–01.00 Sun–Thur, 12.00–03.00 Fri & Sat ⓝ Tram: Muntplein

Nam Kee £ ⓫ One of the city's best-known Chinese restaurants, located in the red light district but popular with Dutch and Chinese locals and tourists alike. ⓐ Zeedijk 111–113 ① 020 624 3470 ⓦ www. namkee.nl ① 12.00–23.00 daily ⓝ Tram: Dam; metro: Nieuwmarkt

Sherpa £ ⓬ Run by a Nepali, this colourful, simple restaurant offers the best Nepalese and Tibetan food in town. Though within a stone's throw of the touristy Leidseplein, it's often overlooked, which keeps prices reasonable. ⓐ Korte Leidsedwarsstraat 58

⬤ *The secluded Kapitein Zeppos restaurant*

ⓣ 020 623 9495 ⓦ www.sherpa-restaurant.nl ⓛ 16.00–23.00 daily
ⓝ Tram: Leidseplein

Kantjil and de Tijger £–££ ⓭ There are countless cheap and
cheerful Indonesian places in Amsterdam, but choose this one if
you want to be guaranteed some of the city's best ethnic food. It's
always full, so you may have to wait for a table. ⓐ Spuistraat
291–293 ⓣ 020 620 0994 ⓦ www.kantjil.nl ⓛ 12.00–23.00 daily
ⓝ Tram: Spui

Me Naam Naan £–££ ⓮ Thai standards such as Pad Thai and Tom
Yam soup and an array of traditional curries pack in the crowds, so
book in advance to avoid a long wait. ⓐ Koningsstraat 29 ⓣ 020 423
3344 ⓦ www.menaamnaan.nl ⓛ 17.00–22.30 daily ⓝ Metro:
Nieuwmarkt

Supper Club ££–£££ ⓯ Part restaurant, part club and a totally unique
dining experience, the Supper Club has live or recorded music, images
projected on to its white walls, changing themes and mattresses to
lounge on while you eat. The set meal is served by attractive young
waiters and waitresses and lasts about four hours. The food is good
rather than brilliant and it's not cheap, but it is a unique night out.
ⓐ Jonge Roelensteeg 21 ⓣ 020 344 6400 ⓦ www.supperclub.nl
ⓛ 20.00–01.00 ⓝ Tram: Dam

d'Vijff Vlieghen £££ ⓰ d'Vijff Vlieghen (The Five Flies) is named after
the five 17th-century canal houses through which its nine dining
rooms sprawl. It serves traditional Dutch food with a modern twist.
Quite formal, but the old-fashioned atmosphere is very romantic
too, so save it for an intimate treat. Reservations recommended.

Spuistraat 294–302 ☎ 020 530 4060 🌐 www.thefiveflies.com
🕐 18.00–22.00 🚊 Tram: Spui

BARS & CLUBS

Bitterzoet Club? Bar? Theatre? Experience? Bitterzoet is all of these things, so check out what's happening in its intimate performing space. You might get a DJ or a drama, maybe a film or even poetry. ☎ Spuistraat 2 ☎ 020 421 2318 🌐 www.bitterzoet.com 🕐 20.00–03.00 Sun–Thur, 20.00–04.00 Fri & Sat 🚊 Tram/metro: Centraal Station

Café Belgique A beer-lover's paradise, with over 50 Belgian brews all available in one place. Serves snacks too. ☎ Gravenstraat 2 ☎ 020 625 1974 🌐 www.cafe-belgique.nl 🕐 14.00–01.00 daily 🚊 Tram/metro: Centraal Station

Grand Café Dulac More bar than café, despite the name, this place is popular with locals rather than tourists. Look out for the stuffed alligators. ☎ Haarlemmerstraat 118 ☎ 020 624 4265 🕐 15.00–01.00 daily 🚊 Tram/metro: Centraal Station

Panama Amsterdammers like their multimedia venues, bringing the spirit of the 1960s into the 21st century. The Panama, in an old power station in the docks to the east of Centraal Station, is one of the best of these. There's a bar/restaurant as well as a club and a theatre space. Most nights there's live music at 21.00, then DJs with themed music nights from 23.00 until late. ☎ Oostelijke Handelskade 4 ☎ 020 311 8686 🌐 www.panama.nl 🕐 Restaurant: 12.00–24.00; club: hours vary 🚊 Tram: Rietlandpark

Eastern Canal Ring & Plantage

If you head to the eastern side of the city, usually referred to as the Eastern Canal Ring and the city district of Plantage, you'll see a very different side of Amsterdam to that which most tourists experience. Visitors with limited time on their hands naturally focus on the centre and the big museums. If you're lucky enough to have more time, or just don't like going where everyone else goes, head east.

Here you'll find some of the greenery the city centre lacks, like the large Oosterpark and the Hortus Botanicus. There are some smaller museums, too, which are worth a visit, as well as the city zoo, Amsterdam's most photographed bridge and – Amsterdam wouldn't be Amsterdam without it – the Heineken Experience.

SIGHTS & ATTRACTIONS

Artis Zoo

The name of Amsterdam's zoo comes from its Latin motto *natura artis magistra* (nature, the mistress of the arts). This grand old zoo dates back to 1838, although in recent years a lot of work has been carried out to modernise the place and give the animals more space and more natural living conditions.

The zoo covers 14 hectares (34 acres) of land and holds 6,000 animals. It's a good idea, therefore, to get a map and decide what interests you most. The African savannah is a popular feature, as are the South American pampas, the renovated aquarium and the wolf enclosure. Check out the feeding times, too, for tamer creatures like penguins and sea lions as well as for the wilder vultures and crocodiles. ❸ Plantage Kerklaan 38–40 ❶ 0900 278 4796 Ⓦ www.artis.nl ❶ 09.00–17.00 (Nov–Mar);

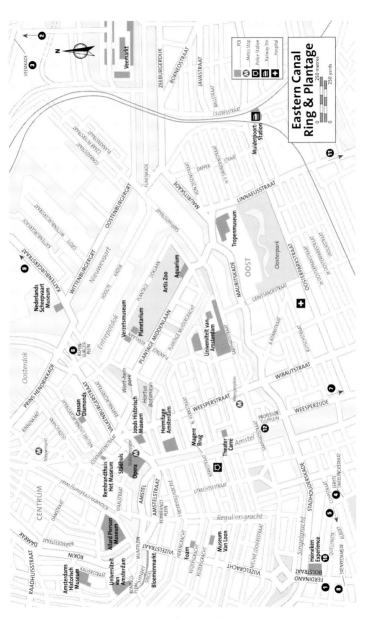

Eastern Canal Ring & Plantage

09.00–18.00 (Apr, May, Sept & Oct); open until sunset June–Aug
Tram: Plantage Kerklaan Admission charge

Entrepotdok

Entrepotdok is one of the first and best examples of the way
Amsterdam's docks, fallen into dereliction, have been developed over
the last few decades and turned into fashionable apartments, bars
and restaurants. This was originally a 'free port' in the dock system,
where goods could be moved in and out without incurring taxes
because they were technically not brought ashore in the Netherlands.
It was the biggest warehouse complex in Europe, built by the Dutch
East India Company in the 1820s. Today it's a lovely and peaceful
place to wander around, still full of character and history. Next
to Artis Zoo Tram: Plantage Kerklaan

Gassan Diamonds

This is one of the best of the many diamond-factory tours. At Gassan,
housed in an impressively old building from 1897, you are given a good
free tour of the cutting and polishing rooms, and the guides are
keen to explain the world of diamonds to you. At the end you sit
around a table as the guide shows you different kinds of diamonds.
You can ask as many questions as you like without necessarily buying.
Of course they'd love it if you did, and many visitors do. Nieuwe
Uilenburgerstraat 173–175 020 622 5333 www.gassandiamonds.com
09.00–17.00 daily Tram/metro: Waterlooplein

Hortus Botanicus (Botanical Gardens)

You don't normally think of botanical gardens as places of great
historical interest, but this one goes right back to 1638 when
Amsterdam began a collection of herbal plants. They were moved

⬥ *The redeveloped Entrepotdok area*

● *Doing the up and under at Magere Brug*

here in 1682, and it's a fabulous place to escape to for a while. You could almost be transported to tropical Asia, from where many of the plants originally came, brought back by the Dutch East India Company from their trade expeditions to the Spice Islands and beyond.

The collection now ranges from Arctic plants in the outdoor gardens to collections of orchids, cacti and palm trees in some of the greenhouses. There's a beautiful butterfly house too and an elevated walkway taking you through a rainforest canopy. ● Plantage Middenlaan 2A ● 020 625 9021 ● www.dehortus.nl ● 09.00–17.00 Mon–Fri, 10.00–17.00 Sat & Sun (Sept–June); 09.00–19.00 Mon–Fri, 10.00–19.00 Sat & Sun (July & Aug) ● Tram: Plantage Kerklaan ● Admission charge

Magere Brug

The so-called 'Skinny Bridge' is one of those sights in Amsterdam that are loved by locals and tourists alike. It is a simple but pretty bridge across the Amstel river that seems to sum up the look of the city. The current bridge dates back to 1670, but has been renovated since then. The story goes that it replaced an earlier and even skinnier bridge across the river, built by two sisters who lived on opposite sides and got tired of the long walk round whenever they wanted to see each other. Their surname, allegedly, was *Magere*, meaning 'skinny'. It's a nice story, true or not, and even if you only spend five minutes here taking the obligatory photo it's an essential Amsterdam highlight. ➋ Between Kerkstraat & Nieuwe Kerkstraat ⓜ Tram/metro: Waterlooplein or Oosteinde

CULTURE

Foam

A centre for independent and contemporary photography and documentary, this small museum of all things photographic has put Amsterdam on the international map. With exhibits ranging from well-known photographers to emerging talent, you can easily lose hours in this place. ➋ Keizersgracht 609 ➊ 020 551 6500 ⓦ www.foam.org ➊ 10.00–18.00 Sat–Wed, 10.00–21.00 Thur & Fri ⓜ Tram: Keizersgracht ➊ Admission charge

Joods Historisch Museum (Jewish Historical Museum)

Some people think that Amsterdam's Jewish connection starts and ends with Anne Frank, but there is a reason the Frank family were hiding here. The city has a long Jewish history. This enterprising museum, which reveals this past, is housed in four

HEINEKEN EXPERIENCE

The Heineken Experience is housed on the grounds of the company's former brewery, where Heineken was made from 1864 until 1988, and is one of the city's most popular attractions. It is no longer a working brewery but offers tours in which you can learn how the brewing process works, follow the life of a bottle of Heineken, watch old television advertisements and meet the company's shire horses. It's all done very professionally, with liberal doses of humour, and the admission charge goes to charity. Allow a couple of hours at least, depending on how long you want to spend sampling the product at the end. You get three free samples of the beer as part of the tour.

Note that the Heineken Experience is immensely popular and queues start forming before it even opens. Visit is by tour only and there are a limited number of tours per day, each taking only so many people. If you don't get there early, you can face a very long wait or you may not get in at all. ⓐ Stadhouderskade 78 ⓣ 020 523 9666 ⓦ www.heinekenexperience.com ⓛ 11.00–19.00 daily (last ticket sales 17.30) ⓜ Tram: Stadhouderskade
ⓘ Admission charge

converted synagogues that date back to the 17th and 18th centuries. The old alleyways and streets of the Jewish quarter have not been lost completely, but were used by the architects and cleverly incorporated into the building's design. As well as focusing on the German occupation of the city, there are international exhibitions of historic and modern Jewish art and artists. ⓐ Nieuwe Amstelstraat 1 (entrance south side of JD Meijerplein, opposite Waterlooplein)

🕿 020 531 0310 🌐 www.jhm.nl 🕐 11.00–17.00 daily 🚇 Tram/metro: Waterlooplein or Mr. Visserplein ❶ Admission charge

Museum Van Loon

This late 17th-century canal house was owned from 1884 to 1945 by the Van Loon family, one of whose ancestors was a founder of the Dutch East India Company. Although Willem van Loon didn't live here at the time, it gives a good impression of what a rich merchant's life would have been like. The opulence of the rooms and the furniture, the marble staircase and the huge collection of family portraits all paint a picture of a life of luxury and privilege. It's a rare chance to look into one of these grand canal homes. Don't forget to check out the garden as well. ⓐ Keizersgracht 672 🕿 020 624 5255 🌐 www.museumvan loon.nl 🕐 11.00–17.00 Wed–Mon 🚇 Tram: Keizersgracht ❶ Admission charge

Nederlands Scheepvaart Museum (Dutch Maritime Museum)

The story of how Amsterdam turned from a little fishing village into the richest port in the world is wonderfully told in this maritime museum, housed in what was once a naval dockyard. There is an enjoyable film about the rise and fall of the Dutch East India Company and at the front of the museum is a replica of a spice-trading ship. As you can see, the romance of the sea wasn't quite so apparent if you were below decks. The ship is a fully working replica and occasionally sets sail to visit other venues, so check if it'll be in port when you are. ⓑ Kattenburgerplein 1, off Kattenburgerstraat 🕿 020 523 2222 🌐 www.scheepvaartmuseum.nl 🕐 10.00–17.00 Tues–Sun (mid-Sept–mid-June); daily (mid-June to mid-Sept) 🚇 Tram/metro: Centraal Station or Kattenburgerstraat ❶ Admission charge

HERMITAGE AMSTERDAM
You don't need to go to Russia to see the world-renowned collections of St Petersburg's Hermitage Museum. Just head to the old Amstelhof nursing home buildings on the Amstel, which is a satellite of the famous Russian art museum. Various exhibitions from its huge and impressive collection are displayed here throughout the year. ⓐ Amstel 51 ① 020 530 7488 ⓦ www.hermitage.nl ⓛ 10.00–17.00 Thur–Tues, 10.00–20.00 Wed ① Admission charge

Tropenmuseum (Museum of the Tropics)
A study of the tropical regions of the world is an unusual theme for a museum in the Netherlands, you might think, but don't forget the Dutch have long had links with, and even ruled, tropical places such as Suriname, Indonesia and several Caribbean islands. The museum sprang out of that history but now takes in the rest of the tropical world. You can walk through an Arab souk and an African village as well as learn about the spice trade. The 19th-century building looks imposing from the outside, but the interior is cleverly designed to include lots of light and space. If you're with children, don't miss the Tropenmuseum Junior or Kindermuseum (Children's Museum).
ⓐ Linnaeusstraat 2 ① 020 568 8200 ⓦ www.tropenmuseum.nl ⓛ 10.00–17.00 ⓝ Tram: Linnaeusstraat ① Admission charge

Verzetsmuseum (Dutch Resistance Museum)
If you tour the Anne Frank House in Amsterdam – and most first-time city visitors do – you should also visit the Resistance Museum. It is equally moving and paints a broader picture of what happened

in the city during the Nazi occupation from 1940 to 1945. Amsterdam had by far the biggest Jewish community in the Netherlands and experienced some of the greatest suffering. Anne Frank was just one of thousands of people hidden from the Germans by Amsterdam's brave citizens, who risked their own lives in order to save others. It is their story that is told here: both those who survived and those who didn't. ❷ Plantage Kerklaan 61 ❶ 020 620 2535 ❿ www.verzetsmuseum.org ❶ 10.00–17.00 Tues–Fri, 11.00–17.00 Sat–Mon ❷ Tram: Plantage Kerklaan ❶ Admission charge

RETAIL THERAPY

This is a terrific area for markets. If visiting the Oosterpark or Artis Zoo, take a detour to the **Dappermarkt** (❷ Dapperstraat ❶ Mon–Sat). At one end it's a general street market comprising mainly clothes stalls. Further on it turns into a food market with lots of ethnic produce. It's colourful and lively and there are lots of food shops lining the same street.

In the very southern end of this quarter of the city, beyond the Heineken Experience, the district known as De Pijp has one of the biggest and best street markets in the city. The **Albert Cuypmarkt** (❿ www.albertcuypmarkt.com ❶ Mon–Sat ❷ Tram: Stadhouderskade or Albert Cuypstraat) sprawls over several streets and sells clothes, general household goods and food from all over the world, reflecting the multicultural make-up of Amsterdam.

There's also the **Waterlooplein Flea Market** (❶ 10.00–17.00 Mon–Sat ❷ Tram/metro: Waterlooplein), alongside the Amstel and very close to Museum Het Rembrandthuis . Here you can buy souvenirs, CDs, paintings, antiques, funky clothes and jewellery, not to mention second-hand clothes and bric-a-brac.

Finally there's the **Bloemenmarkt** (Flower Market ⓐ Singel, near Muntplein ⓒ 09.30–17.00 Mon–Sat, 12.00–17.00 Sun ⓝ Tram: Muntplein or Koningsplein). If you want tulips from Amsterdam, this is the place to get them, along with a wide range of other blooms from the fertile flower-growing fields of the Netherlands. Even if you're not buying, the market makes for a great photo opportunity.

TAKING A BREAK

De Taart van m'n Tante £ ❶ A kitsch café serving stylish *ooh la la* cakes, this little place is full of locals eagerly sinking their teeth into colourful confectionery. ⓐ Ferdinand Bolstraat 10 ⓣ 020 776 4600 ⓦ www.detaart.com ⓒ 10.00–18.00 daily ⓝ Tram: Ferdinand Bolstraatt

Café Kanis & Meiland £–££ ❷ This excellent *eetcafé* in the redeveloped dockland to the east of Centraal Station is a mix of bar and restaurant, with a lovely terrace overlooking the water. ⓐ Levantkade 127 ⓣ 020 418 2439 ⓦ www.kanisenmeiland.nl ⓒ 10.00–01.00 Sun–Thur, 10.00–03.00 Fri & Sat; kitchen open 10.00–22.00 daily ⓝ Bus: 32 to KNSM-Eiland

De Odessa £–££ ❸ Enjoy the novelty factor of eating on a Ukrainian fishing boat. Moored behind a shopping centre in Amsterdam's docks, the Odessa is quirky and hip, with DJs spinning after 22.00 and food and drinks served most of the day. ⓐ Veemkade 259 ⓣ 020 419 3010 ⓦ www.de-odessa.nl ⓒ 16.00–01.00 Wed & Thur, 16.00–03.00 Fri & Sat, 14.00–01.00 Sun ⓝ Tram: Rietlandpark

AFTER DARK

RESTAURANTS

Badcuyp £ ❹ A centre for live world music, Badcuyp boasts an organic *eetcafé* with friendly staff, healthy, delicious food and a pleasant atmosphere. 🅐 Eerste Sweelinckstraat 10 🅣 020 675 9669 🅦 www.badcuyp.nl 🅛 11.00–21.00 Tues–Thur, 11.00–03.00 Fri & Sat 🅣 Tram: Stadhouderskade or Van Woustraat

Cambodja City £ ❺ Serves a fantastic range of dishes from Thailand, Vietnam and Cambodia. Also does takeaways. 🅐 Albert Cuypstraat 58–60 🅣 020 671 4930 🅛 17.00–23.00 Tues–Sun 🅣 Tram: Albert Cuypstraat

Kilimanjaro £–££ ❻ This long-standing African restaurant has some unusual dishes, including antelope and crocodile, with plenty of choice for vegetarians too. Reservations recommended. 🅐 Rapenburgerplein 6 🅣 020 622 3485 🅛 17.00–22.00 Tues–Sun 🅣 Tram: Mr. Visserplein

Girassol ££ ❼ Friendly, family-run Portuguese restaurant with a terrace overlooking the Amstel. Good fresh fish and a reasonably priced wine list. 🅐 Weesperzijde 135 🅣 020 692 3471 🅦 www.girassol.nl 🅛 12.00–22.00 🅣 Tram/metro: Wibautstraat

Olive & Cookie ££ ❽ An intimate restaurant that gives vegetarian food a good name. Friendly, affordable and with great service to match its food. Don't miss out on the cakes! 🅐 Saenredamstraat 67 🅣 020 470 7190 🅦 www.oliveandcookie.com 🅛 16.00–21.00 Mon–Fri 🅣 Tram: Weteringcircuit

Fifteen ££–£££ ❾ Jamie Oliver's Dutch outpost offers exceptional food, great service and a top-notch waterfront location.
ⓐ Jollemanhof 9 ❶ 0900 343 8336 Ⓦ www.fifteen.nl ❶ 12.00–15.00, 17.00–01.00 Mon–Sat, 17.30–01.00 Sun; kitchen open until 22.00
Ⓝ Tram: Kattenburgerstraat

Mamouche ££–£££ ❿ North African couscous, lamb and fish tagine dishes. Reservations are a must. ⓐ Quellynstraat 104
❶ 020 673 6361 Ⓦ www.restaurantmamouche.nl ❶ 18.00–23.00
Ⓝ Tram: Weteringcircuit

De Kas £££ ⓫ Some of the finest food in the city, served either in the spacious dining room or outdoors next to the herb gardens.
ⓐ Kamerlingh Onneslaan 3 ❶ 020 462 4562 Ⓦ www.restaurant dekas.nl ❶ 12.00–14.00, 18.30–22.00 Mon–Fri, 18.30–22.00 Sat
Ⓝ Tram: Hogeweg

La Rive £££ ⓬ Arguably the best restaurant in the city, with two Michelin stars and prices to match. Reservations essential.
ⓐ Amstel Intercontinental Hotel, Professor Tulpplein 1 ❶ 020 520 3264
Ⓦ www.restaurantlarive.com ❶ 12.00–14.00, 18.30–22.00
Mon–Fri, 18.30–22.00 Sat Ⓝ Tram/metro: Weesperplein

BARS & CLUBS
There's no lack of clubs in this area – ask around or look out for flyers.

Brouwerij 't Ij Look for the windmill to find this microbrewery with its no-frills (and no-food) tasting room and roof terrace.
ⓐ Funenkade 7 ❶ 020 622 8325 Ⓦ www.brouwerijhetij.nl
❶ 15.00–20.00 daily Ⓝ Tram: Hoogte Kadijk

Café de Druif This cosy, atmospheric brown café has watched boats and people coming and going since 1631. ⓐ Rapenburgerplein 83 ⓘ 020 624 4530 ⓛ 11.00–01.00 Sun–Thur, 11.00–02.00 Fri & Sat ⓦ Metro: Nieuwmarkt

Escape Amsterdam's largest venue, Escape can accommodate a few thousand clubbers each night. The regular Saturday Framebusters is a huge draw, as is Sundae's (naturally on Sundays) with its Ibiza vibe. Dress smart. ⓐ Rembrandtplein 11 ⓘ 020 622 1111 ⓦ www.escape.nl ⓛ 23.00–01.00 Sun–Thur, 23.00–03.00 Fri & Sat ⓦ Tram: Rembrandtplein

● *The dining room at Fifteen*

Museum district

Sooner or later, every visitor to Amsterdam makes it to what's popularly known as the Museum district, the area surrounding the huge Museumplein.

On the square itself you'll find the big two attractions, the **Rijksmuseum** and the **Van Gogh Museum** which will close for six months of renovation works in September 2012; some works will remain on view during the renovations. The Rijksmuseum is undergoing long-term renovation in several phases and some parts of the huge rambling interior may be closed when you visit, although major exhibitions and collections remain open where possible. The **Stedelijk Museum** is also undergoing maintenance work, but is continuing with temporary exhibitions in which selections from its collections are presented in innovative ways that work with and around the current condition of the building. At the time of writing, no date has been set for the museum's full reopening. Close by there are slick diamond factory tours at **Coster Diamonds**, as well as the hugely popular **Vondelpark**, one of the biggest green spaces within easy reach of the city centre.

The Museum district itself is also an interesting part of the city, – more than just a place which happens to house museums. The tunnel that splits the Rijksmuseum in two had a major road running through it until as recently as the 1990s, when the square, Amsterdam's largest, was turned into a miniature park. While it still has the feel of an artificially made place, it's much more pleasant than it used to be. At one corner, you'll find a small area for skateboarders, and at the far end, people like to congregate on the roof of supermarket Albert Hein, which was built into a man-made hill.

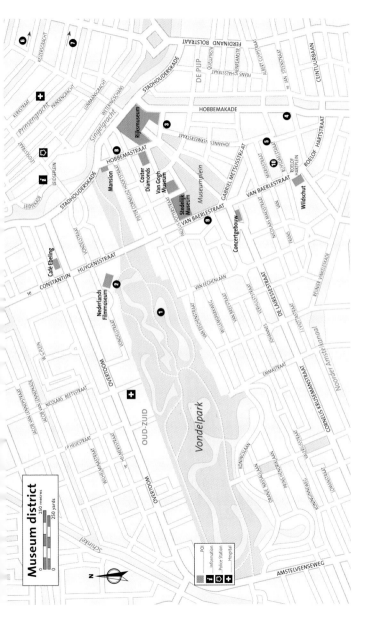

Museum district

0 ——— 250 metres
0 ——— 250 yards

N

POI
Information
Police Station
Hospital

Vondelpark

OUD-ZUID

Schinkel

AMSTELVEENSEWEG

Noorder Amstel kanaal

Streets and locations

KEIZERSGRACHT
KERKSTRAAT
LIJNBAANSGRACHT
PRINSENGRACHT
Prinsengracht
Singelgracht
Singelgracht
STADHOUDERSKADE
WETERINGSCHANS
LEIDSEPLEIN
LEIDSEKADE
STADHOUDERSKADE

FERDINAND BOLSTRAAT
DE PIJP
FRANS HALSSTRAAT
KWISTVERSTRAAT
HENRIKKADE
ALBERT CUYPSTRAAT
1e JAN STEENSTRAAT
CEINTUURBAAN

HOBBEMAKADE
HOBBEMASTRAAT
Rijksmuseum
VERMEERSTRAAT
JOHANNES VERHULSTRAAT
GABRIEL METSUSTRAAT
ROELOF HARTSTRAAT
ROELOF HARTPLEIN
Wildschut
VAN BAERLESTRAAT
NICOLAAS MAESSTRAAT
FRANS
VAN
JAN LUYKENSTRAAT

Coster Diamonds
Van Gogh Museum
Stedelijk Museum
Museumplein
PAULUS POTTERSTRAAT
PIETER CORNELISZOON HOOFTSTRAAT
Mansion

Concertgebouw

Café Ebeling
CONSTANTIJN HUYGENSSTRAAT
1e CONSTANTIJN
VONDELSTRAAT

Nederlands Filmmuseum

VONDELSTRAAT
OVERTOOM
W.G. PLEIN
1e NICOLAAS BEETSSTRAAT
JACOB VAN LENNEPKADE
JACOB VAN LENNEPSTRAAT
J P HEIJESTRAAT
WILHELMINASTRAAT
1e HELMERSSTRAAT
OVERTOOM

VAN EEGHENLAAN
VAN EEGHENSTRAAT
VONDELKERKSTRAAT
VAN BREESTRAAT
EMMASTRAAT
JOHANNES VERHULSTRAAT
VERVERSTRAAT
1e JAN VAN DER HEIJDENSTRAAT
NICOLAAS MAESSTRAAT
DE LAIRESSESTRAAT
TINTORETTOSTRAAT
REINIER VINKELESKADE

KONINGINNEWEG
ORANJE NASSAULAAN
EMMASTRAAT
KONINGSLAAN
CORNELIS KRUSEMANSTRAAT
VALERIUSSTRAAT
CORNELIS SCHUYTSTRAAT

SIGHTS & ATTRACTIONS

Coster Diamonds

This is one of the busiest of Amsterdam's diamond factories, thanks to its proximity to the two main museums and thanks also to its coach-parking facilities. Coach groups do tend to get the attention of the tour guides and individual visitors might find themselves squeezed out or waiting longer than usual for the next tour to start, so if you see several coaches lined up outside it may be better to come back at another time. Free tours run roughly every half hour in summer (hourly in winter), although this varies depending on availability of guides for the different languages catered for.

The tour teaches you about the history of the diamond trade and explains why Amsterdam is one of the world's main diamond

● Find out about Amsterdam's diamond trade at Coster Diamonds

centres. Watch diamonds being polished, learn the grades that exist and why some stones cost more than others. You'll also see the skilled cutters and polishers perfecting the raw material, known as the 'rough'. At the end comes a close encounter with diamonds and jewellery, and, of course, a chance to buy. ➌ Paulus Potterstraat 2–8 ➊ 020 305 5555 ➍ www.costerdiamonds.com ➌ 09.00–17.00 daily ➍ Tram: Hobbemastraat or Museumplein

Vondelpark

Amsterdammers are exceedingly fond of the Vondelpark and make full use of its 45 hectares (111 acres) all year round and especially in summer. Each year more than eight million people visit the park, which has been providing green relief to the city dwellers ever since it opened in 1865. The park is the biggest in the city and is filled with trees, pathways, ponds and lakes teeming with wildlife, children's playgrounds, a bandstand, a rose garden and the **Nederlands Filmmuseum** (➊ 020 589 1400 ➍ www.eyefilm.nl). There are regular concerts in the bandstand in summer and activities for children on Wednesday afternoons.

The park is named after Joost van den Vondel, a popular Dutch poet who lived from 1587 to 1679. Originally it was only 4 hectares (10 acres), designed in the then-fashionable English style for city parks. It proved so popular it was extended to its present size in 1877.

The Filmmuseum, which as well as being a museum is a good place to hang out, sometimes hosts free outdoor films on a summer Saturday night. The rest of the year it shows films of all kinds, in the original language, from Charlie Chaplin through to the latest releases. The museum is due to move to a new location by the IJ river in late 2011. ➌ Information Centre: Vondelstraat 69 ➌ Dawn to dusk ➍ Tram: Leidseplein or Overtoom

CULTURE

Concertgebouw (Concert Hall)

The Concert Hall is worth a look even if you don't enjoy classical music. It has been the home of the Royal Concertgebouw Orchestra since 1888 and in that time some great names, including Mahler, Ravel and Richard Strauss, have conducted here. The building has some of the best acoustics in the world and if you fancy going to a concert, check the website or call in for details. The Concertgebouw tries to be accessible to everyone, offering inexpensive concerts on Sunday mornings and Saturday matinees. There is also often a summer series of cheaper performances. There are two halls inside. Try to get a ticket for the main *Grote Zaal* (Great Hall) if you can, rather than the *Kleine Zaal* (Small Hall), used for recitals.
ⓐ Concertgebouwplein 2–6, off De Lairessestraat ⓣ 020 671 8345
ⓦ www.concertgebouw.nl ⓥ Tram: Museumplein

Rijksmuseum

The Rijksmuseum is the major national art gallery of the Netherlands. The grand building, which opened in 1885, was designed by Petrus Josephus Hubertus Cuypers, the architect who produced Centraal Station. A lengthy refurbishment means that some rooms will be closed (in phases) and the main collection will be rotated into other areas. Works are expected to finish sometime in 2013. This is no reason not to pay a visit, however. In some ways this is even better than visiting the whole museum, as you'll see the best exhibits gathered together in the same space – a truly rich collection.

In one room currently open to the public, you can admire 17 works by Rembrandt. The most important piece in the Rijksmuseum, Rembrandt's *The Night Watch*, is displayed in a separate room. This monumental canvas is so huge and powerful that it will stop you in your tracks. Some of the artist's self-portraits, which show his transition from youth to old age, are among the finest ever painted. You almost expect him to move, to breathe or to start a conversation. A visit here, as well as to Museum Het Rembrandthuis (see page 69), will give you a unique insight into the artist and his work.

The other great Dutch name in the collection is Vermeer, whose works are also kept on show in this temporary display. The best-known is *The Kitchen Maid*, a beautifully lit portrait of a young woman pouring milk into a bowl. Other Dutch Masters whose works can be seen include Jan Steen and Frans Hals. On display you'll find fine arts items alongside the Old Masters, including some wonderful delftware porcelain. ⓐ Jan Luijkenstraat 1 ⓣ 020 674 7000 ⓦ www.rijksmuseum.nl ⓛ 09.00–18.00 Sat–Thur, 09.00–21.30 Fri ⓝ Tram: Museumplein or Hobbemasstraat ⓘ Admission charge

⬤ *The Rijksmuseum*

VAN GOGH MUSEUM

The Van Gogh Museum is the single most visited attraction in Amsterdam. This isn't surprising as it is a delightful museum featuring the finest collection of works by one of the world's best-known artists. It contains about 200 paintings, almost 600 drawings and 700 original letters, mostly written by Vincent van Gogh to his brother Theo. There's also a collection of works by contemporaries of Van Gogh and by people who influenced him or were influenced by him. Names here include Toulouse-Lautrec, Monet, Pissarro and Gaugin, who lived with Van Gogh in France for two months.

The artist's self-portraits are arguably the most striking exhibits. He stares out of the canvas at you unflinchingly. With several portraits displayed side by side it can be an unnerving experience to look back at them. One display shows the oriental work that influenced Van Gogh and hints at the sensitive and delicate side of this mad, misunderstood genius.

There are four floors altogether, plus an annexe. The collection is so large that some of the minor works, such as the drawings, are displayed on a rotating basis. There are also temporary exhibitions. The main attractions, which include popular paintings such as *Wheatfield with Crows*, *The Potato Eaters*, *The Yellow House* and one of the *Sunflowers* paintings, are usually on display unless a special exhibition sees them out on loan.

Allow time to visit the excellent museum shop. Posters are especially popular and come in distinctive triangular cartons that you'll see people carrying all over the city. Go here for tasteful souvenirs, stationery and books, or pick up novelty items such as Van Gogh fridge magnets.

The building is light, airy and spacious, which does help it to cope well with its many visitors. If you don't like crowds, try to get there 15–20 minutes before the doors open or for the last hour or so in the day. Still allow plenty of time, however, to see everything before it closes. Visiting at less busy times of year, such as in the winter, is also recommended. ⓐ Paulus Potterstraat 7 ☎ 020 570 5200 Ⓦ www.vangogh museum.nl ⏰ 10.00–18.00 Sat–Thur, 10.00–22.00 Fri Ⓝ Tram: Museumplein or Hobbemastraat ❶ Admission charge. Closed for renovation Sept 2012–Feb 2013: see website for details

◢ The Van Gogh Museum

Stedelijk Museum

The city's modern art museum, which focuses on art from the late 19th century onwards, is undergoing major renovation works, with no reopening date confirmed at the time of writing. In the meantime, however, it is continually putting on temporary exhibitions that make reference to the museum's peripatetic existence over the past few years.

The collection is focused on modern art and artists, and, although there are some great names here, there are also some interesting lesser-known works. The Stedelijk has three Van Goghs along with works by Picasso, Renoir and Cézanne, Andy Warhol and Willem de Kooning. Temporary exhibitions range from photography and video installations through to multimedia works, from the brilliant to the obscure. ⓐ Paulus Potterstraat 13 ⓣ 020 573 2911 ⓦ www.stedelijk.nl ⓛ 10.00–17.00 Tues–Sun (until 22.00 Thur) ⓝ Tram: Museumplein or Hobbemastraat ⓘ Admission charge. Call ahead to confirm reopening

RETAIL THERAPY

Pieter Cornelisz Hooftstraat Known as PC Hooftstraat, this swish street between the Museumplein and the Vondelpark contains some of the most expensive shopping in the city. Names like Gucci, Armani, Versace, Cartier and Louis Vuitton rub shoulders with the best Dutch designers, surrounded by some smart cafés and restaurants. ⓝ Tram: Museumplein or Hobbemastraat

Van Gogh Museum Shop Only accessible from the museum, and not to be confused with the separate shop that's halfway between here and the Rijksmuseum (though this too is excellent), the Van Gogh Museum Shop has one of the best selections of gifts in the city for those of an artistic bent. Posters are popular but only the start of it. ⓐ Paulus Potterstraat 7 ⓣ 020 570 5200 ⓦ www.van goghmuseum.nl ⓛ 10.00–18.00 Sat–Thur, 10.00–22.00 Fri ⓝ Tram: Museumplein or Hobbemastraat

TAKING A BREAK

The restaurant inside the Van Gogh Museum is very good, with snacks and drinks available all day, hot meals at lunchtime and a special dinner on a Friday evening when the museum stays open late.

't Blauwe Theehuis £ ❶ You'll find this lovely 1930s café in the Vondelpark. It has a large terrace and serves food from breakfast onwards. Upstairs, there's a smarter, if tiny, bar and restaurant with DJs some weekend evenings. ⓐ Vondelpark 5 ⓣ 020 662 0254 ⓦ www.blauwetheehuis.nl ⓛ 09.00–22.30 Mon–Thur, 09.00–24.00 Fri & Sat, 09.00–22.00 Sun

Café Vertigo £ ❷ This terrific place is part of the Filmmuseum, overlooking the Vondelpark. It's ideal for a snack and a drink outside on sultry nights, or for a romantic candlelit dinner. Menus change according to the films being shown at the museum, so expect anything from Hollywood to Bollywood. ⓐ Vondelpark 3 ⓣ 020 612 3021 ⓦ www.vertigo.nl ⓛ 11.00–01.00 daily

Cobra Café £ ❸ Right on the Museumplein, this newish place is named after the CoBrA expressionist art movement – and the striking décor reflects this. It has floor-to-ceiling glass walls, giving you good views across the square and of the street entertainers in

the area. The food is simple but the atmosphere is relaxing.
ⓐ Hobbemastraat 18 ⓣ 020 470 0111 ⓦ www.cobracafe.com
ⓛ 10.00–22.00 daily ⓝ Tram: Museumplein or Hobbemastraat

AFTER DARK

RESTAURANTS

Pheun Thai £ ❹ As usual, if you want a good, cheap meal in a pricier part of the city look to the ethnic restaurants. This is more like a café but the food is fabulous. Also sells takeaway. ⓐ Hobbemakade 71
ⓣ 020 427 4537 ⓛ 17.00–22.00 daily ⓝ Tram: Roelof Hartplein or Hobbemastraat

Eetcafé Loetje £–££ ❺ This steakhouse/bar is very close to the Museumplein and is well worth seeking out. Often packed and always buzzing, it serves daily specials and has a conservatory restaurant. ⓐ Johannes Vermeerstraat 52 ⓣ 020 662 8173
ⓦ www.cafeloetje.nl ⓛ 11.00–24.00 Mon–Fri, 17.00–24.00 Sat
ⓝ Tram: Roelof Hartplein

Kitsch £–££ ❻ True to its name, this hip little place is full of atmosphere. The menu is amusing but good, with healthy portions and great value for money. Only go if you can handle disco, ABBA and dated MTV videos running in the background. ⓐ Utrechtsestraat 42
ⓣ 020 625 9251 ⓦ www.restaurant-kitsch.nl ⓛ 18.00–23.00
Mon–Thur, 18.00–24.00 Fri & Sat (Sept–July); 18.00–23.00 Wed & Thur, 18.00–24.00 Fri & Sat (Aug) ⓝ Tram/metro: Waterlooplein

Pata Negra £–££ ❼ A bustling tapas bar, this place serves great sangria – and tapas, once they arrive. Come here if you're looking for

🔵 *Amsterdammers relaxing at 't Blauwe Theehuis*

good food and a lively night out, but be warned that the busier it gets, the more chaotic the service. ⓐ Utrechtsestraat 124 ☎ 020 422 6250 🌐 www.pata-negra.nl 🕐 12.00–24.00 daily Ⓜ Tram: Fredricksplein

Sama Sebo ££ ❼ Allegedly the best Indonesian restaurant in town. Go for the 20-dish *rijsttafel*, or pick a pavement table in summer for people-watching on the most fashionable shopping street in the city. ⓐ PC Hooftstraat 27 ☎ 020 662 8146 🕐 09.00–01.00 Mon–Sat Ⓜ Tram: Leidseplein or Hobbemastraat

Brasserie Keyzer ££–£££ ❾ If you want an old-fashioned Dutch restaurant, formal and grand with waiters dressed as they were when the place opened in 1905, then the Keyzer is it. You can eat more cheaply in the more casual café at the front, but be prepared to shell out if you book the restaurant. ⓐ Van Baerlestraat 96 ⓣ 020 675 1866 ⓦ www.brasseriekeyzer.nl ⓛ 08.00–24.00 Mon–Sat, 09.00–24.00 Sun ⓝ Tram: Van Baerlestraat

Le Garage £££ ⑩ Definitely the place for a blow-out treat, Le Garage is as fashionable as it gets in Amsterdam. It is a huge converted garage, with mirrored walls and tables, and attracts a smart crowd who pack out the tables tightly wedged against each other. It's a place to dress up for, though if you want to keep it casual there's an annexe called Le Garage en Pluche serving Indonesian-style street food. ⓐ Ruysdaelstraat 54–56 ⓣ 020 679 7176 ⓦ www.restaurant legarage.nl ⓛ 12.00–14.00, 18.00–23.00 Mon–Fri, 18.00–23.00 Sat & Sun ⓝ Tram: Roelof Hartplein

BARS & CLUBS
Mansion A fusion of club, bar and restaurant. The top floor serves modern Chinese cuisine. Below are several bars for lounging in; the ground floor is strictly for dancing. ⓐ Hobbemastraat 2 ⓣ 020 616 6664 ⓦ www.the-mansion.nl ⓛ Restaurant: 19.00–22.30 Tues–Sat; bar: 18.00–01.00 Mon–Thur, 18.00–03.00 Fri & Sat; club: 21.00–03.00 Fri & Sat ⓝ Tram: Hobbemastraat

OCCII This one-time squat at the far end of the Vondelpark has been turned into an alternative venue typical of Amsterdam, with cabaret, theatre and non-mainstream music. Next to the concert hall there's also a restaurant and a sauna. ⓐ Amstelveenseweg 134 ⓣ 020 671 7778 ⓦ http://occii.org ⓛ 21.00–02.00 Sun–Thur, 21.30–03.00 Fri & Sat ⓝ Bus: 62, 142, 170, 171, 172, 197, 370

Paradiso This is mostly a live-music venue, but also hosts club nights with top international DJs and special events. Housed in a former church, it has become an Amsterdam institution and is the city's premier music venue, showcasing 700 artists a year. 🄰 Weteringschans 6 🄲 020 626 4521 🄦 www.paradiso.nl 🄻 Times vary 🄽 Tram: Leidseplein

V Bar & Lounge For a late-night drink in more sophisticated surroundings, the V Bar & Lounge at the Park Plaza Vondelpark Hotel offers a wide range of fine wines by the glass and a bar menu of finger food. Its stylish, contemporary design still manages to include some private corners for quiet chat, while a real fireplace adds a touch of old-fashioned Amsterdam charm. 🄰 Park Plaza Vondelpark, Koninginneweg 34–36 🄲 020 644 6111 🄦 www.parkplaza.com 🄻 11.00–01.00 daily 🄽 Tram: Emmastraat

Wildschut This grand Art Deco café bar is on a square of equally grand buildings, with a terrace enabling you to enjoy them as Amsterdammers have done for more than 80 years. It's often difficult to get a table in summer, because it's always jammed with everyone from bohemians to businessmen. On cold evenings the inside is cosy, with some intimate little booths where you can enjoy a simple meal. Snacks and drinks are served all day, but it's a terrific spot for a nightcap and is popular with audiences from the Concertgebouw a few blocks away. 🄰 Roelof Hartplein 1–3 🄲 020 673 8622 🄻 09.00–24.00 Mon–Fri, 10.00–03.00 Sat & Sun 🄽 Tram: Roelof Hartplein

Western Canal Ring

This area west of the city centre has everything from the brash Leidseplein, a Dutch version of London's Leicester Square or New York's Times Square, through to the picturesque canals of the Jordaan district. On the edge of the Jordaan is one of the city's major attractions, the Anne Frank House.

The Jordaan, which makes up the northern end of this district, used to be a working-class neighbourhood. It then became a bohemian hangout and has subsequently turned into one of the most fashionable areas of the city. It hasn't lost its bohemian feel, though, and its pretty appearance makes it very popular with visitors. There are tree-lined canals, brown bars and cafés, quirky shops, people cycling through the streets and photo opportunities galore. It's a great place to stay and there's a good choice of accommodation from the cheap to the chic, from the old to the new. There are plenty of eating places, too, covering all budgets. The nightlife around the Jordaan district tends to consist of a long, leisurely meal or late-night drinks in a neighbourhood bar. If you want nightclub action, head south to the Leidseplein.

SIGHTS & ATTRACTIONS

Anne Frank House

Visiting the house where Anne Frank wrote her famous teenage diaries is one of the most moving of all Amsterdam experiences. The building itself is an old merchant's house, built in 1635. The small rooms and narrow stairs weren't designed to cope with huge numbers of people, so a visit can be slow-moving. Try to be there before it opens – or later in the evening – to miss the crowds; you can also buy your ticket online to save queuing.

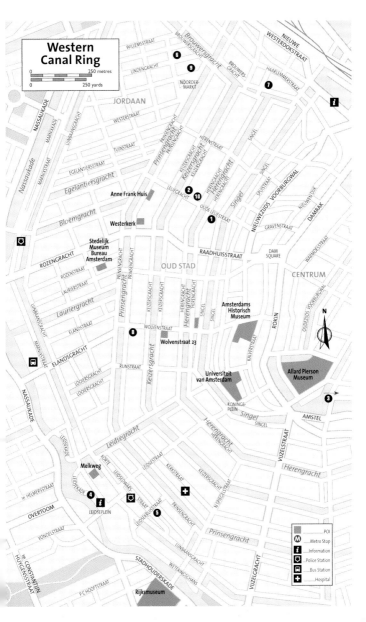

Western Canal Ring

0 — 250 metres
0 — 250 yards

WILLEMSSTRAAT

Brouwersgracht

NIEUWE

WESTERDOKSTRAAT

BROUWERSGRACHT

BROUWERS. GRACHT

6

9

HAARLEMMERSTRAAT

LINDENGRACHT

NOORDER- MARKT

7

SINGEL

i

JORDAAN

WESTERSTRAAT

PRINSENGRACHT

HERENSTRAAT

TUINSTRAAT

KEIZERSGRACHT

KEIZERSGRACHT

KEIZERSGRACHT

PRINSENGRACHT

PRINSENGRACHT

HERENGRACHT

HERENGRACHT

HERENGRACHT

SINGEL

SINGEL

SPUISTRAAT

NIEUWE DIJK

EGELANTIERSSTRAAT

Egelantiersgracht

LELIEGRACHT

2

10

OUDE LELIESTRAAT

1

NIEUWEZIJDS VOORBURGWAL

GRAVENSTRAAT

DAMRAK

Anne Frank Huis

Bloemgracht

Westerkerk

ROZENGRACHT

NASSAUKADE

MARNIXKADE

LIJNBAANSGRACHT

Nassaukade

MARNIXSTRAAT

RAADHUISSTRAAT

DAM SQUARE

WARMOESSTRAAT

M

Stedelijk Museum Bureau Amsterdam

OUD STAD

CENTRUM

ROZENSTRAAT

PRINSENGRACHT

PRINSENGRACHT

KEIZERSGRACHT

KEIZERSGRACHT

HERENGRACHT

HERENGRACHT

HERENGRACHT

SINGEL

SINGEL

OUDEZIJDS VOORBURGWAL

LAURIERGRACHT

Lauriergracht

ELANDSTRAAT

Amsterdams Historisch Museum

N

LIJNBAANSGRACHT

MARNIXKADE

8

WOLVENSTRAAT

ROKIN

P

ELANDSGRACHT

Wolvenstraat 23

KEIZERSGRACHT

RUNSTRAAT

Universiteit van Amsterdam

KALVERSTRAAT

Allard Pierson Museum

LOOIERSGRACHT

LOOIERSGRACHT

KONINGS- PLEIN

3

NASSAUKADE

Leidsegracht

HERENGRACHT

HERENGRACHT

SINGEL

AMSTEL

1e HELMERSSTRAAT

Melkweg

LEIDSEKADE

KORTE LEIDSEDWARS

LEIDSESTRAAT

KERKSTRAAT

KEIZERSGRACHT

N SPIEGELSTRAAT

VIJZELSTRAAT

Herengracht

4

i

5

+

OVERTOOM

LEIDSEPLEIN

LEIDSEKRUISSTRAAT

PRINSENGRACHT

VONDELSTRAAT

Prinsengracht

1e CONSTANTIJN HUYGENSSTRAAT

STADHOUDERSKADE

LIJNBAANSGRACHT

WETERINGSCHANS

VIJZELGRACHT

P C HOOFTSTRAAT

Rijksmuseum

	POI
M	Metro Stop
i	Information
P	Police Station
B	Bus Station
+	Hospital

⬥ *The Anne Frank House – an ordinary façade hides an extraordinary story*

ANNE FRANK

Anne Frank was a Jewish girl unlucky enough to live in the Netherlands during the German occupation of World War II. Born in 1929, she died tragically young in March 1945 in the Nazi death camp at Belsen.

The Frank family had come to Amsterdam from Frankfurt in Germany when Adolf Hitler came to power in 1933. Anne's father Otto Frank began to build up two businesses in the city, one selling herbs and spices and the other producing pectin for jam. Seven years later Hitler invaded the Netherlands. When Anne's sister Margot was called to go to a so-called work project in Germany – in effect a death sentence – Otto Frank took his family into hiding in the tiny rooms above his business premises. They stayed there, crammed together in virtual secrecy, for 25 months. Eventually, they were betrayed to the authorities.

The diary that Anne Frank kept of the family's secret life became an international bestseller and brings millions of people to see the old merchant's house in which she lived. The diary speaks for itself. If you can, read it (or re-read it) just before visiting to get the full emotional impact. You'll probably want to read it again afterwards, too, having seen the place where it was written.

The tour is self-guided and starts with some background exhibitions moving through to the original part of the house where Otto Frank ran his business.

You visit the offices above the workshops, then head up to the annexe where the Frank family lived. It is tiny and has you shaking your head in wonder that eight people could have lived here for over two years almost without detection.

After visiting the secret annexe you move along to more exhibition areas, plus a library where you'll find a nice café to stop and reflect upon your visit. The rooms here have computer displays giving you more information on particular aspects of the house and of the whole Jewish experience during World War II. ❸ Prinsengracht 267 ❶ 020 556 7105 Ⓦ www.annefrank.org ❶ 09.00–21.00, until 22.00 Sat (Mar–Sept); 09.00–19.00, until 22.00 Sat (Oct–Feb); 09.00–22.00 daily (July & Aug) ❶ Tram: Westermarkt ❶ Admission charge

Jordaan district

The best way to visit the Jordaan district is by walking from Centraal Station. It is not too far, although heavy luggage might persuade you otherwise, and it's a great way to introduce yourself to the district.

After the bustle of the station concourse and modern city, the houses become older, quainter and smaller. This was once an overcrowded working-class slum and the size of the buildings along its narrow streets reflects this. Later renovated by an influx of students, artists and entrepreneurs, it's now perfectly picturesque. There are several bridges crossing the canals and in good weather you will see visitors and locals sitting outside the bars and cafés enjoying themselves. Jordaan is the kind of relaxed neighbourhood where you can live like a local. Stop off for a drink, find a favourite spot and you could find you never want to leave.

You might find yourself checking the prices of some of the impressive old canal-side houses, whose tall, elegant lines make the district so attractive. You might wonder what it's like to live on a canal boat, as some people do. Or you might look enviously at one of the old alms houses dotted around the district. These homes,

🔺 *Relax over a drink in the Jordaan district*

called *hofjes*, can be found in courtyards glimpsed from the main streets. Feel free to take a look round, though always remember they are people's homes and not tourist attractions. For a good example of a *hofje* that dates back to 1626, try to find the strangely named Claes Claesz Hofje on Egelantiersstraat (nos 34–54). Claes Claesz was the name of the merchant who founded it.

There are some nice churches here, too – notably the Westerkerk (see opposite) – and some fun markets. However, the Jordaan is above all a place for pleasurable strolling and losing yourself in the cosy atmosphere. Here you can find your own personal piece of Amsterdam.

Leidseplein

There couldn't be more of a contrast to some of the quieter parts of the Jordaan than the brash, busy, neon-lit Leidseplein. It is only neon-lit at night, of course, but that's when most people head for this square and the surrounding streets. They are packed with bars, cafés, restaurants, fast-food places, clubs, cinemas, souvenir shops and the weirdly wonderful Art Nouveau-style **American Hotel**, all stained glass and dark wood (❸ Leidsekade 97 ☎ 020 556 3000 ⓦ www.amsterdamamerican.com). Take a look inside or at least have a drink in the beautifully renovated café, which will take you straight back to the Roaring Twenties.

If you're not into nightlife there's not much to bring you here during the day except for the AUB Ticketshop (see page 28). This sells cheap last-minute tickets for the day's performances at many venues, as well as regular tickets for concerts and plays around the city. Otherwise, relax with a drink at one of the pavement cafés and watch the world go by – quite a show on Amsterdam's Leidseplein. ⓝ Tram: Leidseplein

Westerkerk

The Dutch answer to London's Bow Bells is the Westerkerk, and many people only regard someone as a true Amsterdammer if they grew up hearing its bells. It's the main church in the western part of the city and its lofty tower is visible wherever there is a gap in the tall canal-side buildings. Inside the tower is the heaviest bell in Amsterdam – 7,500 kg (7.39 tons).

The Westerkerk was completed in 1631 and was one of the city's first Protestant churches. It was kept deliberately plain as a reaction against the Catholic inclination towards elaborate design, but is worth visiting for its huge organ and its nave, which is the largest in the Netherlands.

The other notable fact about the church is that it's where Rembrandt was buried in 1669. Don't waste your time looking for his grave, as there isn't one – the artist's burial plot was only rented and his bones were later moved to an unknown location. You will find a plaque on the wall claiming to be the spot where he was originally buried, but even this memorial omits the name by which the artist was known, referring to him only as R Harmensz van Ryn.

Tower tours usually take place in summer only, every hour on the hour from 10.00 to 17.00. It is an awkward climb the higher you get, but make it if you can. It's fascinating to see the nooks and crannies hidden in the tower and at the top, 85 m (279 ft) high, you get the pleasure of probably the finest view of the city, taking in some of its most famous landmarks. Group tours can sometimes be booked outside of regular opening times. ⓐ Prinsengracht 281 ⓣ 020 624 7766 ⓦ www.westerkerk.nl ⓛ Church: 11.00–15.00 Mon–Fri; tower tours hourly 10.00–17.00 Mon–Fri (Apr–Oct) ⓝ Tram: Westermarkt

CULTURE

Stedelijk Museum Bureau Amsterdam (SMBA)

Run by the Stedelijk Museum (see page 100) since 1993, the SMBA serves as multipurpose cultural space putting on a host of temporary exhibitions, lectures, public debates and other events. The main focus is on contemporary art, with around six exhibitions each year. There are frequently artists-in-residence (often international) who offer workshops involving any kind of cultural activity. Best of all, entry to exhibitions and events is generally free of charge. Check the website or call in advance to find out what's on during your stay. ⓐ Rozenstraat 59 ⓣ 020 422 0471 ⓦ www.smba.nl ⓛ 11.00–17.00 Tues–Sun ⓝ Tram: Westermarkt

RETAIL THERAPY

Jordaan, and indeed the whole of the Western Canal Ring, is a shopaholic's heaven. The streets are packed with specialist shops selling antiques, cheese, books, tea, buttons and more; **De Witte Tandenwinkel** (ⓐ Runstraat 5) sells anything and everything to do with teeth, including children's toothbrushes.

In addition there are several markets, with stalls offering anything from conventional fruit and vegetables to bric-a-brac. Head for the **Noordermarkt** in the Jordaan district (ⓐ Boomstraat, just off Prinsengracht ⓛ 09.00–13.00 Mon ⓝ Tram: Westermarkt) for antiques, books, CDs and clothes. The same area on a Saturday hosts an excellent organic food market (ⓛ 09.00–16.00). There's more bric-a-brac of every conceivable description on offer in the huge indoor flea market known as the **Rommelmarkt** (ⓐ Looiersgracht 38 ⓛ 11.00–17.00 daily ⓝ Tram: Elandsgracht).

◢ Visit De Witte Tandenwinkel for all things tooth-related

TAKING A BREAK

Foodism £ ❶ Easily reached from Dam Square, this small, hip restaurant is awash with bright colours. ⓐ Oude Leliestraat 8 ❶ 020 627 6424 ⓦ www.foodism.nl ⓛ 11.30–22.00 Mon–Fri, 11.30–18.00 Sat & Sun ⓝ Tram: Dam

Spanjer & Van Twist £ ❷ Right beside the tranquil Leliegracht canal, this is one of the best *eetcafés* in the city, for both the atmosphere and the food. ⓐ Leliegracht 60 ❶ 020 639 0109 ⓦ www.spanjerenvantwist.nl ⓛ 10.00–01.00 daily ⓝ Tram: Westermarkt

Puccini £–££ ❸ This intimate espresso bar serves delicious breakfasts and lunches. ⓐ Staalstraat 21 ❶ 020 620 8458 ⓦ www.puccini.nl ⓛ 08.30–18.00 Mon–Fri, 10.00–18.00 Sat & Sun ⓝ Tram/metro: Waterlooplein

Café Americain ££ ❹ With its ornate stained-glass chandeliers and vast windows, this Art Nouveau café is a popular meeting point for Amsterdammers. ⓐ Leidsekade 97 ❶ 020 556 3010 ⓛ 06.30–23.30 Mon–Fri, 07.00–23.30 Sat & Sun ⓝ Tram: Leidseplein

AFTER DARK

RESTAURANTS

De Blauwe Hollander £ ❺ Down-to-earth Dutch restaurant near the Leidseplein with large communal tables. Popular with locals. ⓐ Leidsekruisstraat 28 ❶ 020 627 0521 ⓦ www.deblauwehollander.nl ⓛ 12.00–23.00 daily ⓝ Tram: Leidseplein

Tapas Café Duende £–££ ❻ Smoky, atmospheric tapas restaurant with tapas, sangria and flamenco at the back. ⓐ Lindengracht 62 ❶ 020 420 6692 Ⓦ www.cafeduende.nl ❶ 16.00–24.00 Mon–Thur, 16.00–01.00 Fri & Sat Ⓝ Tram: Prinsengracht

De Belhamel ££ ❼ Overlooking the picturesque Herengracht and Brouwersgracht canals, this Art Nouveau restaurant serves seasonal French-Italian cuisine. A bit pricey but worth it for such splendid surroundings. ⓐ Brouwersgracht 60 ❶ 020 622 1095 Ⓦ www. belhamel.nl ❶ 12.00–16.00, 18.00–22.00 (until 22.30 Fri & Sat) Ⓝ Tram: Martelaarsgracht

Van Puffelen ££ ❽ Canal-side brown café/casual restaurant which opens up into a floating barge in summer. ⓐ Prinsengracht 375–377 ❶ 020 624 6270 ❶ 15.00–01.00 Mon–Thur, 13.00–01.00 Fri, 12.00–01.00 Sat & Sun Ⓝ Tram: Westermarkt

Bordewijk £££ ❾ One of Amsterdam's most fashionable eating places, smart but not stuffy. The menu is French fusion with changing accents depending on the season. Reservations recommended – book a table near the window if you can. ⓐ Noordermarkt 7 ❶ 020 624 3899 Ⓦ www.bordewijk.nl ❶ 18.30–22.30 Tues–Sat Ⓝ Tram: Westermarkt

Christophe £££ ❿ If you want to sample the finest of Amsterdam's fine dining, look no further. This place has set high standards since it opened in 1987, and earned its first Michelin star two years later. Dress is smart casual and the food is French gourmet with a touch of North Africa reflecting Christophe Royer's Algerian birthplace. ⓐ Leliegracht 46 ❶ 020 625 0807 Ⓦ www.restaurantchristophe.nl ❶ 18.00–22.30 Tues–Fri, 18.30–22.30 Sat Ⓝ Tram: Westermarkt

BARS & CLUBS

De Admiraal This old tasting house is run by a distillery and is definitely the place to head if you fancy a hard drink and a bit of history. There are usually at least 16 gins and 60 liqueurs on offer. It also serves snacks and proper meals. ⓐ Herengracht 319 ① 020 625 4334 Ⓦ www.proeflokaaldeadmiraal.nl ⓛ 16.30–24.00 Mon–Fri, 17.00–24.00 Sat Ⓝ Tram: Spui

Maloe Melo This place claims to be the home of the blues in Amsterdam, and as such it's this genre that tends to dominate the nightly live shows; however, appearances by soul, jazz, rock 'n' roll or reggae outfits are not uncommon. It's been rocking since 1998 and shows no signs of slowing down! ⓐ Lijnbaansgracht 163 ① 020 420 4592 Ⓦ www.maloemelo.com ⓛ 21.00–03.00 Sun–Thur, 21.00–04.00 Fri & Sat Ⓝ Tram: Elandsgracht

Melkweg This multicultural centre is open all day for exhibitions, dance and theatre events, films and concerts. It's spread over five halls and several rooms of an old dairy factory behind the Leidseplein. At the Marnixstraat entrance you can enjoy basic café dining in Eat@Jo's Café, and browse the free photo gallery while you're there. ⓐ Lijnbaansgracht 234A or Marnixstraat 409 ① 020 531 8181 or 020 638 3336 Ⓦ www.melkweg.nl ⓛ Eat@Jo's: 12.00–21.00 Wed–Sun; photo gallery: 12.00–20.00 Wed–Sun; event hours vary Ⓝ Tram: Leidseplein

▶ *The miniature city of Madurodam*

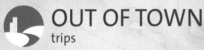
OUT OF TOWN
trips

Den Haag (The Hague)

Known to the world for being the seat of the International Court of Justice, the principal judicial organ of the UN, The Hague is in fact one of the loveliest cities in the Netherlands. It is worth at least a day trip from Amsterdam, or better still an overnight stay if you can afford the time. It's full of museums and beautiful old buildings, and enjoys a lively café, bar and restaurant scene. This mix of old and new makes the city both stimulating and relaxing.

The Hague is the country's governmental hub, housing the Dutch Parliament as well as the Permanent Court of Arbitration and The Hague Academy of International Law. Visit if you're interested in history, politics, architecture or the royal family. If you're looking for a day out shopping, bypass The Hague and go straight to Rotterdam (see page 130), which is further south. Only 20 minutes away by train you'll find Delft, famous for its charming canals and blue and white pottery.

Tourist information office ⓐ Hofweg 1 ❶ 070 361 8860 ⓦ www. denhaag.com ⓝ Tram: 1, 16, 17; bus: 4, 5, 22

GETTING THERE

The Hague is 56 km (35 miles) southwest of Amsterdam. It is an hour away by train and a return ticket costs around €20. Driving, depending on traffic conditions, is usually slightly faster. There is no metro in The Hague so most people get around by tram or bus, both of which operate from directly outside the train station. The OV-*chipkaart*, the same as the one used in Amsterdam (see page 56), is valid here. If you want to reach the centre, get off the train at Centraal rather than Den Haag HS.

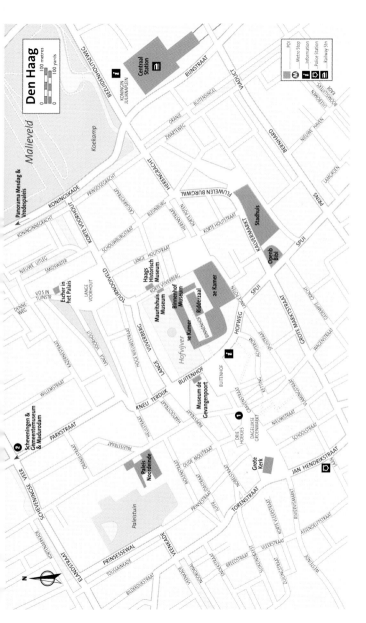

⬤ *The Binnenhof in The Hague*

CAPITAL IDEA
Even though The Hague is not the capital of the Netherlands, it often likes to think it is: it's the home of the Dutch Parliament, the royal family, all of the foreign embassies, and one of the biggest jazz festivals in the world, the **North Sea Jazz Festival** in July (ⓦ www.northseajazz.com).

SIGHTS & ATTRACTIONS

Dutch Parliament Buildings
The 13th-century **Ridderzaal** (Knights' Hall) stands at the centre of the **Binnenhof**, the old Dutch Parliament's Inner Court. Parliament today meets in modern buildings on the south side of the complex, but the Queen still delivers an annual speech from her throne in the **Ridderzaal**. The only way to look around is on one of the regular guided tours, which take 30–45 mins. ⓐ Binnenhof ⓣ 070 364 6144 ⓦ www.binnenhofbezoek.nl ⓛ Tours 10.00–16.00 Mon–Sat ⓝ Tram: 1, 16, 17; bus: 4, 5, 22 ⓘ Admission charge

Madurodam (model town)
A paradoxical place – a vast miniature city encompassing the edited highlights of the Netherlands. From Schiphol Airport to the bulb fields, Delft to Utrecht and The Hague's Peace Palace to Amsterdam's Royal Palace, it's all here compressed on a 1:25 scale. A great place to take the kids. ⓐ George Maduroplein 1 ⓣ 070 416 2400 ⓦ www.madurodam.nl ⓛ 09.00–20.00 daily (Apr–June); 09.00–23.00 daily (July & Aug); 09.00–18.00 daily (Sept–Mar) ⓝ Tram: 9; bus: 22 ⓘ Admission charge

> **THE HEDGE**
> The Hague's unusual name 'Den Haag' (The Hedge) dates back almost 800 years. The Ridderzaal (see page 123) that was built here in the 13th century was once the home and seat of government of the counts of Holland. Prior to its construction, the counts had a hunting lodge on the same site, which was surrounded by a hedge. The city that grew up around the castle was called 's Gravenhage ('the count's hedge', the connotation being that it was a private enclosure). Over time, this was simplified to Den Haag.

Museum de Gevangenpoort (Prison Gate)

The collection of torture instruments and the torture room always get people's attention here, but there's a lot more to see in this 15th-century former prison. There are guided tours in various languages throughout the year. Long-term renovations are currently ongoing but museum staff still offer guided historical walking tours around other areas of the city. Call in advance to check. ⓐ Buitenhof 33 ① 070 346 0861 Ⓦ www. gevangenpoort.nl ① 10.00–17.00 Tues–Fri, 12.00–17.00 Sat & Sun; last tour 16.00 Ⓝ Tram: 1, 16, 17; bus: 4, 5, 22 ① Admission charge

Scheveningen

It only takes about 15 minutes on a tram to get to this beach resort, which is a suburb of The Hague. Take the chance to relax by walking along the beach, admiring the pier and the grand old seafront buildings or visiting the aquarium. Ⓝ Tram: 1

🔺 *The Hague is a lively mix of old and new*

Vredespaleis (UN International Court of Justice)

The Hague is the seat of the International Court of Justice, also known as the Peace Palace. It's an impressive building, founded in 1899 and paid for by the American philanthropist Andrew Carnegie. There are guided tours of the buildings when the courts are not in session, so check and book a tour in advance if you want to visit.
ⓐ Carnegieplein 2 ❶ 070 302 4242 Ⓦ www.vredespaleis.nl
ⓛ Tours: 10.00, 11.00, 14.00 & 15.00 Mon–Fri, 16.00 Sat & Sun
Ⓝ Tram: 1; bus: 4, 13 ❶ Admission charge

CULTURE

Escher in het Palais (Escher in the Palace)

The Lange Voorhout Palace in the old city centre was once a royal palace. Inside it these days you'll find the world's biggest collection of work by the Dutch graphic artist Maurits Cornelis Escher. Almost everything he ever produced is housed here, including his famous 'impossible' works, such as *Waterfall*, where water appears to flow uphill. The café, set in the former Queen's kitchen, is also good.
ⓐ Lange Voorhout 74 ❶ 070 427 7730 Ⓦ www.escherinhetpaleis.nl
ⓛ 11.00–17.00 Tues–Sun Ⓝ Tram: 16, 17; bus: 4, 5, 22 ❶ Admission charge

Gemeentemuseum (Municipal Museum)

This is the city's main art and crafts museum, housing works by Picasso, Kandinsky and leading 20th-century Dutch artist Piet Mondriaan. There's some Delft pottery and local silver, for which The Hague is well known. You'll also find collections of musical instruments, fashion and photography, with changing temporary exhibitions.
ⓐ Stadhouderslaan 41 ❶ 070 338 1111 Ⓦ www.gemeentemuseum.nl
ⓛ 11.00–17.00 Tues–Sun Ⓝ Tram: 17; bus: 4, 14 ❶ Admission charge

Haags Historisch Museum (Historical Museum)

The highlight of this well-presented historical museum is its series of temporary exhibitions, exploring colourful and unexpected aspects of Dutch history, such as its influence on the growth of Indonesian rock music or aboriginal art. The semi-permanent collection, covering the story of The Hague, its govenment and inhabitants from the 1600s to the present day, is dry but informative. ⓐ Korte Vijverberg 7 ⓣ 070 364 6940 ⓦ www.haagshistorischmuseum.nl ⓛ 10.00–17.00 Tues–Fri, 12.00–17.00 Sat & Sun ⓝ Tram: 10, 16, 17 ⓘ Admission charge

Mauritshuis Museum

Works by artists from Rembrandt to Andy Warhol are on display in this stunning neoclassical building next to the Binnenhof, including Warhol's portrait of Queen Beatrix. Vermeer's *View of Delft* and *Girl with a Pearl Earring* offer a bit of a contrast and there are also paintings here by Rubens, Van Hals, Jan Steen and Van Dijck. ⓐ Korte Vijverberg 8 ⓣ 070 302 3435 ⓦ www.mauritshuis.nl ⓛ 10.00–17.00 Tues–Sat, 11.00–17.00 Sun ⓝ Tram: 10, 16, 17 ⓘ Admission charge

Panorama Mesdag

This unusual attraction has to be seen to be believed. It's a 360° cylindrical painting of the sand dunes at the nearby seaside resort of Scheveningen (see page 124), which you can stand inside. It's about 14 m (46 ft) high and was produced by the noted 19th-century local artist Hendrik Willem Mesdag. ⓐ Zeestraat 65 ⓣ 070 364 4544 ⓦ www.panorama-mesdag.com ⓛ 10.00–17.00 Mon–Sat, 12.00–17.00 Sun & public holidays ⓝ Tram: 1; bus: 4, 5, 22 ⓘ Admission charge

TAKING A BREAK

RESTAURANTS

't Goude Hooft ££ ❶ An inn dating from 1492 (though its current home was built in the 1930s) with a fabulous central location. Classic Dutch dishes include potato croquettes, pea soup with sausages, and apple tart. ⓐ Dagelijkse Groenmarkt 13 ❶ 070 346 9713 ⓦ www.tgoudehooft.nl ❶ 08.00–01.00 Mon–Sat, 10.00–24.00 Sun

Ramakien ££ ❷ *The* place for authentic Thai cuisine, serving dishes cooked lightly but full of flavour and spice. Excellent fish. It's slightly far out of the centre but worth the walk or taxi ride: follow Parkstraat north to Alexanderstraat, then turn left into Laan van Meerdervoort. ⓐ Laan van Meerdervoort 542C, corner Goudenregestraat ❶ 070 356 2352 ⓦ www.thai4you.nl ❶ 17.00–23.00 Wed–Mon ⓝ Tram: 12

AFTER DARK

BARS & CLUBS

De Paap Not to be confused with De Paas, De Paap is a café bar with live gigs by emerging new bands. The whole of this street is a trendy place to go at night. ⓐ Papestraat 32 ❶ 070 365 2002 ⓦ www.naastdepaap.nl ❶ 17.00–late Wed–Fri, 14.00–late Sat & Sun ⓝ Tram: 2, 16

Paard van Troje Offering everything from funk, dance hall and jazz to ska music and stand-up comedy, this venue – whose name means 'Trojan horse' – can house up to 1,100 party people and has showcased top acts such as Kane and DJs Deep Dish. It's the perfect place to try out your dancing shoes. ❷ Prinsengracht 12 ❶ 070 360 1838 Ⓦ www.paard.nl ● Times vary

De Paas One of The Hague's best brown cafés, with a great selection of over 150 beers – definitely worth the walk. Follow Wagenstraat southeast to find Dunne Bierkade. ❸ Dunne Bierkade 16A ❶ 070 360 0019 Ⓦ www.depaas.nl ● 15.00–01.00 Sun–Thur, 15.00–01.30 Fri & Sat

ACCOMMODATION

For further advice on accommodation in The Hague and to make reservations, contact the **tourist office accommodation department** (❶ 070 338 5815 Ⓦ www.denhaag.com).

Hotel des Indes ££ One of the best-value 5-star hotels in town. Visiting VIPs stay here all the time. ❸ Lange Voorhout 54–56 ❶ 070 361 2345 Ⓦ starwoodhotels.com Ⓝ Tram: 9 plus a short walk

Hotel Mimosa £ Inexpensive family hotel right by the sea in Scheveningen. Perfect for a cheap, quick break and a breath of fresh seaside air. ❸ Renbaanstraat 18–24 ❶ 070 354 8137 Ⓦ www.hotel mimosa.nl Ⓝ Tram: 1, 9; bus: 22

Rotterdam

Lying 26km (16 miles) south of The Hague, Rotterdam is the Netherlands' second-biggest city and is very different from the capital. In some ways it's less exciting, but in others it's fresher and funkier – a 'Manhattan on the Maas'. It also seems much bigger, because the centre sprawls whereas Amsterdam is kept compact by its canals.

Rotterdam, with its imposing skyline that dominates the landscape for miles around, is the place to go for stunning modern architecture, museums and shopping. Its port, one of the biggest and busiest in the world, is also an incredible sight. Considered Amsterdam's younger, more commercial sister, the city boasts an international population and follows a faster rhythm of life. One potential drawback – most people who work here live in the suburbs, making the city surprisingly quiet at night.

Tourist information office ⓐ Stationsplein 45 ⓣ 010 271 0120 ⓦ www.rotterdam.info ⓛ 09.00–17.30 Mon–Sat, 10.00–17.30 Sun ⓜ Metro: Stadhuis

GETTING THERE

Rotterdam boasts a wide network of motorways and roads and an extensive public transportation system. Rotterdam Centraal Station is a major hub in the Dutch railway network and there are six direct connections to Amsterdam every hour. Travel time is an hour and a quarter and a return ticket costs around €25. Rotterdam is also just 15 minutes from The Hague by train.

Eurolines coaches do travel to Rotterdam, but are much slower than the train and do not stop in the centre. Traffic tends to be heavy both in the city centre and on the outskirts.

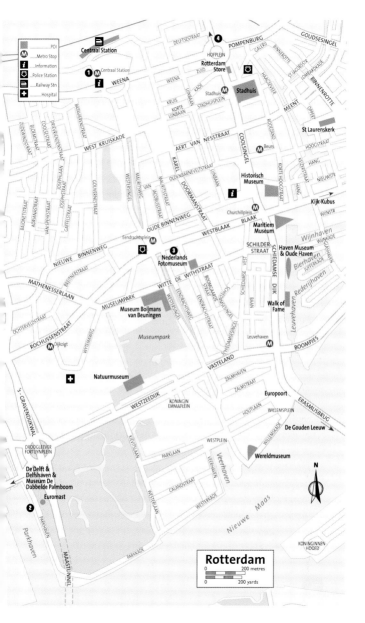

Rotterdam

0		200 metres
0		200 yards

N

SIGHTS & ATTRACTIONS

De Delft & Delfshaven

Go back in time and watch *The Delft*, a fantastic 18th-century shipwreck being reconstructed in a shipyard. On board this ongoing reconstruction you can see not only the treasures that were recovered but also the craftsmen at work on their various specialist tasks. There are great waterfront views, too, and a chance to see the area known as Delfshaven. This was originally the port for Delft and has survived as a wonderful old quarter of Rotterdam, with a definite maritime atmosphere and plenty of cafés and bars. ⓐ Schiehaven 15 ⓣ 010 276 0115 ⓦ www.dedelft.nl ⓛ 10.00–16.00 Wed–Fri, 11.00–17.00 Sat & Sun Ⓝ Tram: 8

Euromast

If you've no head for heights, this sight is not for you. The Euromast first takes you to a height of 100 m (328 ft), where there's a breathtaking view of Rotterdam and its vast harbour, a brasserie-style restaurant, and even two luxury suites. For the brave, you can then take a ride to the very top on the rotating Euroscoop lift, 185 m (607 ft) in the air. ⓐ Parkhaven 20 ⓣ 010 436 4811 ⓦ www.euromast.nl ⓛ 09.30–23.00 daily (Apr–Sept); 10.00–23.00 daily (Oct–Mar) Ⓝ Tram: 8; metro: Dijkzigt ⓘ Admission charge

Guided tours of the ports

The best way to see the vast port of Rotterdam, which is truly incredible, is on the Spido boat. The harbour tour lasts about 75 minutes and an introductory DVD sets the scene. As well as seeing the harbour you get excellent views of some of the city's quirky architecture. Tours and day trips during July and August

range from 75 minutes to seven hours. ⓐ Willemsplein 85 (at the base of the Erasmus Bridge) ⓣ 010 275 9988 ⓦ www.spido.nl
ⓝ Tram: 7; metro: Leuvehaven

Haven Museum & Oude Haven

The older parts of Rotterdam's extensive docks are here at Oude Haven, along with a great indoor/outdoor working museum that really gives you a feel for life in the shipyards over the years. Old boats are restored here and you can also take a steamboat ride out into the harbour. ⓐ Leuvehaven 50–72 ⓣ 010 404 8072
ⓦ www.havenmuseum.nl ⓛ 09.00–17.00 daily ⓝ Tram: 1, 8, 20; bus: 32, 49; metro: Beurs or Churchillplein

Historisch Museum (Historical Museum)

Housed in the only remaining 17th-century building in Rotterdam, this museum tells the story of the city's history using everything from domestic artefacts to grand documents. There's an extensive print and sketch collection. ⓐ Korte Hoogstraat 31 ⓣ 010 217 6767
ⓦ www.hmr.rotterdam.nl ⓛ 11.00–17.00 Tues–Sun ⓝ Tram: 1, 8, 20, 23; metro: Beurs ⓘ Admission charge

Maritiem Museum (Maritime Museum)

This museum really does Rotterdam's impressive maritime history justice. The interactive exhibits, including a 15-m (49-ft) model of the modern port, are impressive and there are lots of activities for children. ⓐ Leuvehaven 1 ⓣ 010 413 2680 ⓦ www.maritiem museum.nl ⓛ 10.00–17.00 Tues–Sat, 11.00–17.00 Sun & public holidays; also open 10.00–17.00 Mon (July–Aug & school holidays)
ⓝ Tram: 1, 8, 20; bus: 32, 49; metro: Beurs or Churchillplein
ⓘ Admission charge

◯ *Rotterdam's wacky Cube Houses*

ARCHITECTURE

Rotterdam has become renowned for its startling modern architecture, which manages to combine the Dutch flair for quirky originality with stylish modern concepts. Simply walking around the city is an experience, as you never know what you are going to see. The simple Euromast thrusts into the air like an Olympic torch and down at the harbour you can see a building that seems to lean over at an alarming angle. It's the KPN Telecom building, designed by Renzo Piano, the man who came up with the inside-out Pompidou Centre in Paris.

The best-loved examples of Rotterdam's architecture are probably the fun-looking **Kijk-Kubus** (Cube Houses ⓐ Overblaak 70 ❶ 010 414 2285 Ⓦ www.kubuswoning.nl 🕐 11.00–17.00 daily Ⓝ Tram: 21; metro: Rotterdam Blaak). It is hard to see how people can actually live in these angled cubes supported by a few poles. Fortunately, one is open for visitors.

To see this and other examples of Rotterdam's unique buildings, it's worth taking an organised Architecture Tour, which you can book through the tourist office or a travel agent.

Museum De Dubbelde Palmboom (History Museum)

This 19th-century warehouse in the old port at Delfshaven houses a museum focusing on Rotterdam's history as a port and on the human side of the city's past. The personal stories are truly compelling. ⓐ Voorhaven 12 ❶ 010 476 1533 Ⓦ www.dedubbelde palmboom.nl 🕐 11.00–17.00 Tues–Sun Ⓝ Tram: 4, 8 ❶ Admission charge

Natuurmuseum

This villa houses an old-fashioned natural history museum, displaying mostly stuffed animals and birds, some beautiful butterflies and a number of scary bugs. The highlight is the 15-m (49-ft) skeleton of a sperm whale. ⓐ Westzeedijk 345, Museumpark ⓣ 010 436 4222 ⓦ www.nmr.nl ⓛ 10.00–17.00 Tues–Sat, 11.00–17.00 Sun ⓝ Metro: Eendrachtsplein ⓘ Admission charge

CULTURE

Museum Boijmans van Beuningen

The city's main art museum has a fine collection, ranging from the Old Masters to modern works by artists such as Kandinsky, Dalí and Magritte. There are also pieces by Van Gogh, Gaugin, Monet, Dégas, Titian, Rembrandt, Breughel and Hieronymus Bosch. ⓐ Museumpark 18–20 ⓣ 010 441 9400 ⓦ www.boijmans.rotterdam.nl ⓛ 11.00–17.00 Tues–Sun ⓝ Tram: 5 ⓘ Admission charge

Nederlands Fotomuseum

The Dutch haven't earnt a reputation for photography, but this national museum suggests that they could. It has an archive of about four million negatives from more than 80 of the country's leading photographers, displayed on a rotating basis. There are also temporary photography exhibitions. ⓐ Wilhelminakade 332, corner Witte de Withstraat & Eendrachtstraat ⓣ 010 203 0405 ⓦ www.nederlandsfoto museum.nl ⓛ 10.00–17.00 Tues–Fri, 11.00–17.00 Sat & Sun ⓝ Tram: 5, 8

Wereldmuseum

The roots of this fascinating museum, which has been recently renovated, hail from the spice trade, when Dutch sailors brought back interesting objects from Indonesia. There is now a collection of more than 200,000 items celebrating arts and crafts all over the world. There are especially good displays on Islamic and Aboriginal arts, and the 19th-century photographic archive is impressive.

ⓐ Willemskade 25 ⓣ 010 270 7172 ⓦ www.wereldmuseum.com
ⓛ 10.00–20.00 Tues–Sun ⓝ Tram: 7
ⓘ Admission charge

RETAIL THERAPY

Rotterdam is a great place for fashion enthusiasts. You'll find stylish boutiques, stores, cafés and gift shops in the area between Kruiskade and Van Oldenbarneveltstraat, close to Centraal Station. If you're looking for top-brand men's and women's footware, try **Shoebaloo** (ⓐ Kruiskade 57C ⓦ www.shoebaloo.nl ⓛ 12.00–18.00 Mon, 10.00–18.00

🔺 *Rotterdam is brilliant for shopping*

Tues–Thur & Sat, 10.00–21.00 Fri, 12.00–17.00 Sun). Another great area for shopaholics is Hillegersberg, just north of the city centre.

Rotterdam has the largest market square in the Netherlands, the **Binnenrotte** (🕐 09.00–17.00 Tues & Sat (Jan–Apr); 09.00–17.00 Tues, Sat & Sun (May–Dec), which is filled with around 500 stalls selling all sorts of food and drink, plants, fresh flowers and second-hand goods.

Rotterdam is such a hotspot for shoppers that the tourist board even puts out a special booklet with eight shopping routes you can do on foot. These include the historic part of the city, near the waterfront, the hip and freaky and the chic. It's worth picking one up.

TAKING A BREAK

RESTAURANTS
Grandcafé-Restaurant Engels ££ ❶ Whatever food you're in the mood for you'll find it here in the renovated Groothandelsgebouw. It now boasts an American-style bar, a tapas restaurant, and the Grand Café itself, where you can have everything from a coffee and a light snack to a three-course meal with wine. ⓐ Groothandelsgebouw, Stationsplein 45 ☎ 010 411 9550 ⓦ www.engels.nl 🕐 08.00–01.00 daily Ⓜ Metro: Centraal Station

Pancake Boat ££ ❷ What could be more Dutch than eating pancakes on a boat? Once the ship sets sail you can eat your fill of all kinds of flavours available at the buffet. But remember, you've only got an hour. ⓐ Parkhaven, opposite the Euromast ☎ 010 436 7295 ⓦ www.pannenkoekenboot.nl 🕐 Check website or phone for times Ⓣ Tram: 8

Restaurant de Engel £££ ❸ Top international cuisine with a constantly changing menu based on seasonal produce. In addition to the à la carte option, the chef provides daily specials which are also available at lunchtime alongside the very reasonable fixed-price menu. ❷ Eendrachtsweg 19 ❶ 010 413 8256 ❿ www.hermandenblijker.nl ❸ 12.00–14.00, 18.00– 22.00 Mon–Fri, 18.00–22.00 Sat ❷ Metro: Centraal Station

St Paul's £££ ❹ This is allegedly a French restaurant, but its menu is truly international. There are some quirky combinations, such as chicken stuffed with crab and served with a Yorkshire pudding – but usually they work. Sit back and enjoy. ❷ Kleiweg 89 ❶ 010 418 5274 ❿ www.restaurantstpauls.nl ❸ 18.00–22.00 Wed–Sun ❷ Tram: 4; bus: 35, 49

AFTER DARK

BARS & CLUBS
Baja Beach Club Miles from any beach, slap in the middle of the city centre, this club does aim for a beach-party feel. Girls get free champagne all night on the first Tuesday of the month. ❷ Karel Doormanstraat 10–12 ❶ 010 213 1180 ❿ www.baja.nl ❸ 22.30–05.00 Thur–Sun ❷ Metro: Eendrachtsplein

Coconuts A Caribbean-style dance bar/restaurant with a friendly, festive atmosphere. Good cocktail menu and music from DJs. ❷ Stadhuisplien 19 ❶ 010 413 0804 ❿ www.coconuts.nl ❸ 22.00–05.00 daily ❷ Metro: Stadhuis

De Gouden Leeuw Well-established English-style pub with a pool table and basic pub food. It is located quite far southeast of the city centre, so it's best to take the bus or a taxi there.

🅐 Ijsselmondsehoofd 1–3 ☎ 010 482 7569 🕐 11.00–23.00 Mon,
11.00–20.00 Tues–Thur, 11.00–22.00 Fri, 14.00–22.00 Sat Ⓝ Tram: 23;
bus: 183

Paddy Murphy's Not very traditionally Dutch, but with live music
every night of the week, usually until late, this is where lots of
Rotterdammers hang out. Great buzz. 🅐 Rodezand 15 ☎ 010 411 0078
Ⓦ www.paddymurphys.nl 🕐 12.00–late Ⓝ Metro: Beurs

ACCOMMODATION

HOTELS
Maritime Hotel Rotterdam £ Excellent location near the waterfront
if you want to explore the maritime side of the city. A three-star
hotel with 165 rooms and cheap rates, sometimes offering special
deals. 🅐 Willemskade 13 ☎ 010 201 0900 Ⓦ www.maritimehotel.nl
Ⓝ Tram: 7; metro: Leuvehaven

Hotel New York ££ If you can afford to splash out a bit, this 19th-century
head office of the Holland America Line has been transformed into a
modern four-star hotel. 🅐 Koninginnenhoofd 1 ☎ 010 439 0500
Ⓦ www.hotelnewyork.nl Ⓝ Tram: 20

HOSTELS
Stayokay Rotterdam £ Rotterdam's city hostel is very central,
very comfortable and has 100 beds available in single, double and
quadruple rooms. 🅐 Rochussenstraat 107–109 ☎ 010 436 5763
Ⓦ www.stayokay.com Ⓝ Metro: Dijkzigt

⏵ *Amsterdam's excellent tram network makes travelling around the city a pleasure*

PRACTICAL
information

Directory

GETTING THERE

By air

Amsterdam's Schiphol Airport is about 18 km (11 miles) southwest of the city centre and is well served by scheduled flights from all over Europe and beyond. The flight time from London is about 45 minutes.

bmi fly from Belfast, Birmingham and East Midlands ❶ 0870 607 0555 Ⓦ www.flybmi.com

bmibaby fly from Belfast, Birmingham and East Midlands ❶ 0870 264 2229 Ⓦ www.bmibaby.com

British Airways fly from London Heathrow, Gatwick and London City Airport ❶ 0870 850 9850 Ⓦ www.britishairways.com

easyJet fly from Belfast, Bristol, Edinburgh, Glasgow, Liverpool, Manchester and London Stansted, Luton and Gatwick ❶ 0871 244 2366 Ⓦ www.easyjet.com

Jet2 fly from Leeds-Bradford ❶ 0870 737 8282 Ⓦ www.jet2.com

KLM fly from London Heathrow, London City and numerous UK regional airports ❶ 0870 243 0541 Ⓦ www.klm.com

Many people are aware that air travel emits CO_2, which contributes to climate change. You may be interested in the possibility of lessening the environmental impact of your flight through the charity **Climate Care** (Ⓦ www.jpmorganclimate care.com), which offsets your CO_2 by funding environmental projects around the world.

By rail

DutchFlyer offers good-value all-inclusive rail and sail tickets from the UK to Amsterdam. Ⓦ www.dutchflyer.co.uk

Eurostar services to Brussels allow an onward connection direct to

Amsterdam, with a total journey time of 4–6 hours from the UK.
☎ 0870 518 6186 ⓦ www.eurostar.com
There are good rail connections between Amsterdam and many
major continental European cities. See **Rail Europe** ☎ 0870 584 8848
ⓦ www.raileurope.co.uk
The **Thomas Cook European Rail Timetable** has up-to-date
schedules for European, international and national train services.
☎ (UK) 01733 416477 or (USA) 1 800 322 3834
ⓦ www.thomascookpublishing.com

By road
There are ferry services (see page 144) if you wish to take your car to
Amsterdam, and a network of good fast roads from elsewhere in

⬥ *Sunflowers at Schiphol Airport*

🔺 MS Stena Hollandica *docked at the Hook of Holland*

Europe. But Amsterdam's not the best city to explore by car – if it's not essential for your trip, leave it at home.

Eurolines has a daily coach service from London Victoria coach station to Schiphol Airport. ☏ 08717 818181 🌐 www.eurolines.co.uk

By water

To reach Amsterdam by ferry from the UK involves going either to Rotterdam or to the Hook of Holland, then driving or taking an onward rail connection to Amsterdam.

P&O Ferries have daily overnight services from Hull to Rotterdam. ☏ 0870 520 2020 🌐 www.poferries.com

Stena Line sail twice daily from Harwich to the Hook of Holland. ☏ 0870 570 7070 🌐 www.stenaline.com

ENTRY FORMALITIES

Citizens of the UK, Republic of Ireland and other EU countries, the USA, Canada, Australia and New Zealand do not require a visa for stays of up to 90 days in the Netherlands. Citizens from other countries, as well as those wishing to stay longer than 90 days, will require a visa. A valid passport is always necessary.

Visitors to the Netherlands from within the EU are entitled to bring their personal effects and a reasonable amount of alcohol and cigarettes for personal consumption only. Those entering from outside the EU may bring in 200 cigarettes (or 250 grams of tobacco or 50 cigars) and two litres of non-sparkling wine plus one litre of strong spirit or two litres of sparkling or fortified wine.

MONEY

The Dutch currency is the euro (€), divided into 100 cents. Notes are in denominations of 5, 10, 20, 50, 100, 200 and 500; coins in 1 or 2 euros and 1, 2, 5, 10, 20 and 50 cents.

There are numerous banks, ATMs and bureaux de change in central Amsterdam, as well as in Rotterdam and The Hague. While credit cards are widely accepted, many smaller establishments will insist on cash.

TRAVEL INSURANCE

It is strongly recommended that you take out adequate personal travel insurance for the trip, covering medical expenses, loss, theft, repatriation, personal liability and cancellation expenses. If you are travelling in your own vehicle you should also check that you are appropriately insured and have all the relevant documents and your driving licence with you.

HEALTH, SAFETY & CRIME

Tap water in Amsterdam is perfectly safe to drink unless marked otherwise and food hygiene is generally to a high standard. The Dutch healthcare system is first class and EU citizens are entitled to free or reduced-price treatment on production of a valid European Health Insurance Card (EHIC). See Ⓦ www.dh.gov.uk/travellers for more information.

Crime is not a big issue in Amsterdam, although there is a drug problem. Be careful around Centraal Station and the red light district, especially late at night. Also watch out for pickpockets and fraudsters.

There is a useful central **police station** near Leidseplein at ❸ Lijnbaansgracht 219. The headquarters can be found on

🔽 *The Nederlands Scheepvaart Museum in Amsterdam (see page 85)*

Elandsgracht, and other stations are located at ❷ Beursstraat 33,
❸ Nieuwezijds Voorburgwal 104, ❸ Keizerstraat 3 and
❸ Prinsengracht 1109. Call ❶ 0900 8844 to report lost property as
well as more serious theft, assault and hate/discrimination crimes.

OPENING HOURS

Shop opening hours vary. Many stay open longer on Thursdays, then
open later the next morning. It's also fairly common for stores in the
city centre to open on a Sunday afternoon and get off to a leisurely
start on Monday mornings.

Museums are typically open 10.00–17.00, but close on Sunday
mornings and Mondays. Some smaller attractions also close
on Mondays.

Banks normally open 09.00–16.00 Monday to Friday. Some open longer on Thursdays, while others open Saturday mornings instead.

TOILETS

Public toilets are not widespread in Amsterdam. The ones that do exist are usually very clean, but they do carry a small charge. For men there are a limited number of French-style toilets around the streets. Your only real option is to use a bar, café or hotel, though in the first two it is considered polite to buy something.

CHILDREN

Amsterdam is usually thought of as a city for singles, party groups and couples on romantic breaks, but there's plenty for families to do too. Children are welcomed almost everywhere, although you may want to keep them out of the red light district.

In terms of museums and attractions, the interactive science and technology centre NEMO (see page 65) is both educational and entertaining and aimed directly at children. The Tropenmuseum Junior (see page 86) is a section of the Tropenmuseum that teaches children about the cultures of the world.

If you're in Amsterdam for the weekend, plan ahead and book your child into the **Kinderkookkafe** (ⓐ Vondelpark 6B (Overtoom 325) ① 020 625 3257 ⓦ www.kinderkookkafe.nl ⓛ 10.00–17.00 daily ⓝ Tram: Jan Pieter Heijestraat or Overtoom), where they spend Saturday or Sunday afternoon learning to cook, and serve you the finished meal at the end. Or visit the Vondelpark (see page 95), where there are plenty of playgrounds and other activities.

If visiting Rotterdam, don't miss the Maritiem Museum (see page 133), which explores Dutch sea heritage in a way that deliberately provides lots of hands-on activities for children.

🔺 *Kids will enjoy the Maritiem Museum in Rotterdam*

COMMUNICATIONS

Internet

There are several Internet cafés in the city centre.

Easyinternetcafé ⊜ Damrak 33 🕐 09.00–22.00 daily

Internet City ⊜ Nieuwendijk 76 🕐 10.00–24.00 daily

Phone

Most public phone boxes take either credit cards or phonecards. You can buy phonecards in post offices, tourist information centres and tobacconists.

The Netherlands has warmly embraced the mobile phone revolution and a large number of service providers in the UK and other countries have a network available in Amsterdam. You can also buy a SIM card for use in the Netherlands to replace your own while you are away.

TELEPHONING THE NETHERLANDS

To call Amsterdam from overseas, dial the international access code from your country (usually 00), then the code for the Netherlands (31), then the area code without the first zero (eg 20 for Amsterdam or 70 for The Hague). Then dial the number you require, which will usually be another seven digits.

TELEPHONING ABROAD

To call home from Amsterdam, dial the international access code 00, followed by the code for the relevant country. Dialling codes are as follows: UK +44; USA and Canada +1; Australia +61; New Zealand +64; Ireland +353; South Africa +27.

Post

There are plenty of post offices around the city. They are usually open 09.00–17.00 Monday to Friday, with some of the larger offices also open on Saturday mornings. The main post office is at Singel 250 and stays open until 20.00 Monday to Friday. You can buy stamps at post offices, shops or hotels.

ELECTRICITY

Voltage in Amsterdam and throughout the Netherlands is 220V, 50Hz, with plugs being the usual two round-pin continental type. If you need an adapter or a voltage transformer, buy one before leaving home because it will be hard to find one in Amsterdam.

TRAVELLERS WITH DISABILITIES

Amsterdam is not the easiest place to navigate for those with physical disabilities. It's a medieval city with many cobbled streets, narrow pathways and bridges, and the traffic of cars, pedestrians, trams and rapidly moving cyclists is busy. Lots of the buildings are old, narrow and on several floors, so check in advance before booking a hotel.

Metro stations in Amsterdam are equipped with lifts and many new trams and buses are now accessible for wheelchair users. Call **GVB** (see page 52) for details of which lines are equipped. There are also special private wheelchair-accessible taxi services in the city such as **Garskamp** (ⓐ Disketteweg 10 ⓣ 020 633 3943 ⓔ info@ garskamp.nl) and **Connexxion Jonkcars** (ⓣ 020 606 2200); advance booking is recommended. Those visitors with motorised wheelchairs can use the numerous bike paths.

For a good source of travel-related information contact the **ANWB Disabled Department** on ⓣ 070 314 1420 ⓦ www.anwb.nl

TOURIST INFORMATION

The Amsterdam Tourist Board is now known by the trendy name
of **I amsterdam** (☎ 020 201 8800 ⓦ www.iamsterdam.com). There
are several offices in Amsterdam, including in front of Centraal
Station and on Leidseplein. They are generally very good, with lots
of free information and helpful staff who speak several languages.
There is a small fee for booking accommodation or tickets.

Useful websites include:

ⓦ www.aub.nl
ⓦ www.holland.com

BACKGROUND READING

Geert Mak's Amsterdam: A Brief Life of the City by Geert Mak. It is
anything but brief, though never less than fascinating.
The Diary of a Young Girl by Anne Frank. If you have read it already,
read it again.
Outsider in Amsterdam by Janwillem van de Wetering. First in the
excellent crime novel series entitled Amsterdam Cops.
The *Van der Valk* crime novels by Nicolas Freeling are set in Amsterdam.
The *Inspector Dekok* mysteries by A C Baantjer are also good, easy
reads and very atmospheric.

🔺 *A canal in Amsterdam at night*

Emergencies

Freephone number for all emergencies ☎ 112
Call from any phone box, landline or mobile phone. There are
English-speaking operators 24 hours a day.

MEDICAL SERVICES

For 24-hour emergency medical and dental help, call the **Central
Medical Service** (☎ 020 592 3434). English-speaking operators can
tell you which doctors and dentists are on duty, and which of them
speak English. Hotels and pharmacies can also advise.

There is a 24-hour accident and emergency department at the
Onze Lieve Vrouwe Gasthuis hospital (🅰 1E Oosterparkstraat 279
☎ 020 599 9111 🌐 www.olvg.nl).

EMERGENCY PHRASES

Fire!	**Help!**	**Stop!**
Brand!	Hulp!	Stop!
Brant!	*Hul-ep!*	*Stop!*

Call the fire brigade!	**Call the police!**
Bel de brandweer!	Bel de politie!
Bel de brant-vayr!	*Bel de pol-eet-see!*

Call an ambulance!
Waarschuw een ziekenauto!
Vaarskoow an zeeken-owtoe!

Amsterdam has two types of chemist or pharmacy. For general medical supplies and non-prescription drugs go to a *drogist* and for prescription drugs take your prescription to the *apotheek*. These are normally open 08.30–17.30 Monday to Friday. For details of out-of-hours pharmacies see pharmacy windows or the daily newspaper *Het Parool*.

POLICE

In case of theft or other emergencies, the most convenient police station for the city centre is near Leidseplein at ❷ Lijnbaansgracht 219

There are other stations at ❷ Prinsengracht 1109 and ❷ Beursstraat 33. The headquarters, the Hoofdbureau van Politie, is on Elandsgracht. For general enquiries call ❶ 0900 8844

EMBASSIES & CONSULATES

Australian Embassy ❷ Carnegielaan 4, The Hague ❶ 070 310 8200

British Consulate ❷ Koningslaan 44, Amsterdam ❶ 020 676 4343

Canadian Embassy ❷ Sophialaan 7, The Hague ❶ 070 311 1600

New Zealand Embassy ❷ Eisenhowerlaan 77N, The Hague ❶ 070 346 9324

South African Embassy ❷ Wassenaarseweg 40, The Hague ❶ 070 392 4501

United States Consulate ❷ Museumplein 19, Amsterdam ❶ 020 575 5309

ACKNOWLEDGEMENTS

Thomas Cook wishes to thank NEIL SETCHFIELD, to whom the copyright belongs, for the photographs in this book, except for the following images:

BIGSTOCKPHOTO.COM pages 7 (Diego Cervo), 19 (Mark Slusarczyk), 40–41 (Ivonne Wierink), 59 (Natalia Bratslavsky), 146–7 (Eric Gevaert); TRAVIS CRAWFORD page 37; DREAMSTIME.COM pages 9 (Eric Gevaert), 29 (Fairoesh), 33 (Noamfein), 143 (Veniamin Kraskov); WARWICK LISTER-KAYE page 153; MICHEL DE NIJS page 5; PAIGE K PARSONS page 115; PCL TRAVEL pages 20, 81 (AA World Travel Library), 97 (Bruce Yuan-Yue Bi); PHOTOSHOT page 91 (UPPA); STOCKEXPERT.COM page 119 (Jarno Gonzalez); SXC.HU pages 38 (G & A Scholiers), 75 (Ron Beekmeijer); WIKIMEDIA COMMONS pages 99 (Oxyman), 144 (Joop van Houdt).

For CAMBRIDGE PUBLISHING MANAGEMENT LIMITED:
Project editor: Tom Lee
Layout: Donna Pedley
Proofreaders: Kate Taylor & Michele Greenbank

Send your thoughts to
books@thomascook.com

- **Found a great bar, club, shop or must-see sight that we don't feature?**
- **Like to tip us off about any information that needs a little updating?**
- **Want to tell us what you love about this handy little guidebook and more importantly how we can make it even handier?**

Then here's your chance to tell all! Send us ideas, discoveries and recommendations today and then look out for your valuable input in the next edition of this title.

Email the above address (stating the title) or write to:
pocket guides Series Editor, Thomas Cook Publishing, PO Box 227, Coningsby Road, Peterborough PE3 8SB, UK.

WHAT'S IN YOUR GUIDEBOOK?

Independent authors Impartial up-to-date information from our travel experts who meticulously source local knowledge.

Experience Thomas Cook's 165 years in the travel industry and guidebook publishing enriches every word with expertise you can trust.

Travel know-how Thomas Cook has thousands of staff working around the globe, all living and breathing travel.

Editors Travel-publishing professionals, pulling everything together to craft a perfect blend of words, pictures, maps and design.

You, the traveller We deliver a practical, no-nonsense approach to information, geared to how you really use it.

Useful phrases

English	Dutch	Approx pronunciation
BASICS		
Yes	Ja	*Ya*
No	Nee	*Nay*
Please	Alstublieft	*Als-too-bleeft*
Thank you	Dank u wel	*Dank oo vel*
Hello	Dag/hallo	*Dakh/hallo*
Goodbye	Dag/tot ziens	*Dakh/tot zeens*
Excuse me	Pardon	*Par-don*
Sorry	Sorry	*Soree*
That's all right	Dat geeft niet, hoor	*Dat khayft neet, hor*
I don't speak any Dutch	Ik spreek geen Nederlands	*Ik sprayk khayn Nederlands*
Do you speak English?	Spreekt u Engels?	*Spraykt-oo Eng-els?*
Good morning	Goedemorgen	*Khooda-morkha*
Good afternoon	Goedemiddag	*Khooda-middakh*
Good evening	Goedenavond	*Khooda-afont*
Goodnight	Goedenacht	*Khooda-nakht*
My name is ...	Ik heet ...	*Ik hayt ...*
NUMBERS		
One	Een	*Ayn*
Two	Twee	*Tway*
Three	Drie	*Dree*
Four	Vier	*Feer*
Five	Vijf	*Fayef*
Six	Zes	*Zess*
Seven	Zeven	*Zayfen*
Eight	Acht	*Akht*
Nine	Negen	*Naykhen*
Ten	Tien	*Teen*
Twenty	Twintig	*Twintikh*
Fifty	Vijftig	*Fayeftikh*
One hundred	Honderd	*Honderd*
SIGNS & NOTICES		
Airport	Vliegveld	*Fleekh-felt*
Railway Station	Trein Station	*Trayn Sta-syon*
Platform	Spoor/perron	*Spoar/perron*
Smoking/Non-smoking	Roken/Niet Roken	*Roh-keh/Neet Roh-keh*
Toilet	Toilet	*Twa-let*
Ladies/Gentlemen	Dames/Heren	*Daam-es/Heer-ren*
Metro/Tram	Metro/Tram	*Meet-roh/Traam*